Joe Montana's Art and Magic of Quarterbacking

Joe Montana

with Richard Weiner

Henry Holt and Company
New York

To my father, Joe Montana Sr., who was always there, who helped make my life so understandable, and who laid the foundation for all I am thankful. And to all the other fathers who understand the dedication required in the early development of their sons—though the visual reward may not come until some time way down the line.

—*Joe Montana*

To my family, without whom this project would have no meaning. And to Joe, for putting up with me for way too long.

—*Richard Weiner*

Henry Holt and Company, Inc.
Publishers since 1866
115 West 18th Street
New York, New York 10011

Henry Holt® is a registered trademark of Henry Holt and Company, Inc.

Published in Canada by Fitzhenry & Whiteside Ltd.,
195 Allstate Parkway, Markham, Ontario L3R 4T8.

Library of Congress Cataloging-in-Publication Data
Montana, Joe, 1956–   .
    Joe Montana's art and magic of quarterbacking / Joe Montana with Richard Weiner. — 1st ed.
        p. cm.
    ISBN 0-8050-4277-6 (alk. paper)
    1. Montana, Joe, 1956–   . 2. Quarterback (Football)   I. Weiner, Richard, 1961–   .   II. Title.
GV951.3M66   1997
796.332'092—dc21
[B]   97-30517
                                                                                                  CIP

Henry Holt books are available for special promotions and premiums. For details contact: Director, Special Markets.

First Edition 1997

Designed by Trejo Production

Printed in the United States of America
All first editions are printed on acid-free paper.

10 9 8 7 6 5 4 3 2 1

COLLABORATOR'S NOTE

Let's get right to it. There is only one Joe Montana. That was painstakingly clear as I did the research for this project. Over and over people would tell me, "Joe was the only one who could. . . ."

And even Joe, while he would never admit it, knows this is true on many counts. But to stop there would be to fail in the learning process. Why, for instance, do we study great leaders? To say they were the greatest and, therefore, can never be duplicated? No, it is to learn any tidbit that which can help us improve, succeed, or rebound from failure.

That, to me, is what is so special about the following text. Having covered Joe during his championship years in San Francisco for *The Peninsula Times Tribune* of Palo Alto, and later for *The Houston Post* and *The New York Times*, and now having listened to him break down the art and magic of quarterbacking, one theme is clear: Joe has revealed little of this book's information as a player—at least not for public consumption.

Part of that, no doubt, was his continual effort to downplay any accomplishment. He was a living cliché: team game, team guy. As you will see, Joe even admits to taking the blame when there were mishandled snaps from center—no matter whose fault it really was. The other reason, probably, is that Joe never wanted to reveal anything in public—in fear that someone might read and then use it against his team for a victory some day.

Throughout our collaboration, Joe was as prepared as possible. This was his mantra as a quarterback. Yes, Joe had God-given talent. But when Joe speaks of never partying in high school because he was too busy practicing, or the way he visualized his new plays at night, highlighting the path of the ball in red, it also becomes apparent that his consistent All-Star performance was more than athletic giftedness. The consensus of his coaches interviewed for this project was that Joe absorbed information faster than any player.

I learned a lot of what Joe Montana was all about as a quarterback one day on the golf course. He used everything: advice from people stationed at each hole; previous experience on the course; the yard-markers at every stop; the clubs the group ahead of him were using on each tee. Watching him compute the information . . . suddenly, it all became apparent: This is how Joe sized up a defense. He would absorb any information possible. Then go out and execute like none other. Later I asked Joe if he could play golf professionally. He thought for a moment, then said time commitment would be the problem. But that would take away from his newly found home schedule, so don't expect that to happen. However, you can expect to learn something from the following chapters.

True, there will only be one Joe Montana. And there can only be one book of his trade secrets.

—Richard Weiner

FOREWORD

I'll say it without any disclaimer. Joe Montana is the greatest quarterback who ever played the game.

While it's virtually impossible to compare quarterbacks when you're talking about different eras, I still put Joe Montana at the top of the list. A lot of times you'll say about a quarterback, "Well, he won, but he had the great teams." I was talking to Troy Aikman about this recently. He's not going to have the numbers. Aikman's legacy is going to be wins. Dan Marino and John Elway are great ones, but neither of them have won a Super Bowl. Their legacy is going to be numbers. And that would be the group if you had to put together the best of today's quarterbacks—with Steve Young the last few years, and then Brett Favre coming into that group. There's not a whole heck of a lot of them.

Montana's got both the numbers and the wins. But he had to do it the hard way, because he never had a dominant running game. He had to do it without a great, dominant offensive line. He had a good system, and he had Jerry Rice and so on, but I never felt he had dominant players all around him.

Most people know how well Joe Montana has played, the statistics, the big games, the come-from-behinds, the injuries, the Super Bowls. With everything Joe's done, people forget just how hard he prepared. In doing telecasts, I regularly talk with the players involved with each particular game. Joe Montana knew more about football, on offense, than any player I ever talked to. (His teammate with the 49ers, Ronnie Lott, knew more about defense than any player I ever talked to.) Montana made things look so easy and natural that he never got enough credit for how hard he worked and how much he knew about the game. That's the part you never saw. That's the part that always impressed me. And that's the part that was least talked about . . . But, hey, now Joe's decided to tell us.

He'll be taking you through each step of his preparation for a game. Then on game day he'll take you into the huddle, to the line of scrimmage, and into the pocket—the whole art of how to pass, the entire process he went through in reading the defense. He'll tell you about the techniques of dropping back—the 3-step, 5-step, and 7-step drops, and the mechanics of each. When people think quarterbacking, the feet don't always come to mind—but without those mechanics down it's going to be awfully difficult. Some quarterbacks get all tightened up, or they're fighting themselves on their drop-back. They're thinking so much about what they're supposed to be doing with their feet that they can't do much with what they've got in their hands. Joe made it look easy—break the huddle, get up, drop back, read, throw. He just went boom, boom, boom.

And here's why you want to learn how to do these things from someone like Joe—because he wasn't one of those real big, strong-armed guys. Guys like Joe have to do everything right.

And if there's one position in the NFL where doing it right really matters, it's quarterback. In high school, a running game can get you the wins. Same with college. You used to be able to do it to some extent in the NFL. Not anymore. Not by a long shot. What it's come to now—well, you have to be able to throw the ball to win. You have to be able to throw it with accuracy. You have to be able to throw it when you need to against any type of defense.

But you have to go even further back than high school to find where the teaching of a quarterback begins. It started early for Joe, as he'll soon tell you. This book will be a good place to start for the quarterbacks of the draft class of 2010. But even if you don't have aspirations to be a quarterback at any level, you're going to still want to know what Joe Montana has to say about football. Maybe you're a fan who wants to know what it's like to see the game from the inside out. Or maybe Montana's been your guy and you want to know how he did what he did.

Either way, when this guy's got something to say about football, you listen.

—John Madden

CONTENTS

ACKNOWLEDGMENTS

We would like to thank the following for contributions without which this book could not have been completed: Suzette Cox, Coach Ben Parks, Karin Arnold, Robert Yanagi, Jarrett Bell, Michael Silver, Peter King, Rich Rosenbush, Danny DeFreitas, Leonard Koppett, Mike McDevitt, Carrie and Robert Shook, Tony and Carolyn Razzano, Sid Gillman, Tom Martinez, Tyrone Willingham, Keith Peters, Al Davis, John Madden, Gail Prichard, Bill Walsh, Matt Millen, Reggie White, Steve Spurrier, John Barnes, John Nelligan, Harris Barton, Edward DeBartolo Jr., Carmen Policy, Jerry Rice, Jamie David, Buddy Ryan, Sam Wyche, Paul Hackett, Steve Bono, Patrick and David Kinsel, Russ Francis, Steve Atwater, Mary Buck, Lawrence Taylor, Roger Craig, YA Tittle, Johnny Unitas, Sonny Jurgensen, Daryle Lamonica, Paul Warfield, Joe Washington, Oliver Stone, Pete Abitante, Bruce Allen, Rick Gosselin, Timothy Smith, Thomas George, Ed Werder, Ira Miller, Gary Myers, Bob Glauber, Rodney Knox, Dave Rahn, Renaldo Juanso, Peter Brewington, Kelley Snell, Alex Stern, Sandy Montag, Micala Goldberg, Karen Jeffries, Steve and Pauline Belich, Jeff and Sabrina Bayer, and the late Sam Skinner.

We would also like to make a special mention to those whose hands-on work allowed this project to come to life: David Sobel, John Monteleone, Mark Gola, Margaret Trejo, Peter Johnson, Jeff Herman, Matthew J. Lee, Ken Toyama, Robin Pezzimenti, Ralph Hendrickson, Stanford University, and Sir Bubba I.

INTRODUCTION

Performance under extreme pressure.
Extraordinary demands, both mental and physical.
Having to take a hit to make a play, then get back up.

Maybe you think those are reasons *not* to play quarterback. Or maybe they get you fired up just thinking about it. Like most things, it's all in how you look at it. It's not for everyone, but if you like to have your hands on the ball and be responsible for putting it where it belongs, you can't do any better than quarterback. Not that you won't be nervous before games—I *always* was.

Talking up the challenges and rewards of my sport and my position—and helping out aspiring players any way I can—are just a few of the reasons why I wanted to do this book. Here are some others.

I had a lot of great mentors when I was growing up—especially my father, Joe Sr., who made it all possible—but I never had a book about quarterbacking to read. I wish someone had given me one. I never knew what my real strengths were until I made it to the NFL. This book can't take the place of a great relationship with a coach or a parent, but hopefully it can play a part in the development of some young quarterbacks.

You'll be reading a conversation between myself and those quarterbacks, but this is more than just an instructional book for young athletes. I think there is a lot that coaches of young people can gain from this. With my playing days over and four kids whose days are beginning, I have some advice for mothers and fathers of budding athletes, too. A lot of it you'd think would be common-sense, but it must not be. Not when you see so much pressure being put on kids—sometimes to the point that the kids lose their love for the sport. And when you lose that, forget it—especially in a game like football that requires so much personal sacrifice. We all know plenty of examples of young, professional athletes who've been worked too hard too early. Unfortunately, there are plenty more kids who never make it to the professional ranks that have to endure this stuff, too. There are ways to encourage kids without wearing them down. I know, because my parents and coaches were great at that. I'll be letting you know what they did for me.

I also believe that fans will get a lot out of this book. Football is a very misunderstood sport. Because it's so complicated, and because it evokes such fierce loyalties, it can be frustrating for fans. The players may have a whole lot of pressure on them, but at least they can do something about the outcome. The fans want to win almost as badly as the players do, but they can't do anything but sit and watch. Or stand and scream. So the fans sometimes oversimplify things, relying on statistics, for example, to try to get a handle on what's going on. That doesn't always work. I'll give you some things you can watch for on TV that might show you what numbers alone can't.

Fans also expect too much from the quarterback—and heap too much of both credit and blame on him when things go right or wrong. They say not to judge a man until you've walked a mile in his shoes. In this book, I'll help you spend some time in the cleats of a quarterback. When I talk about reading defenses in Chapter 10, that alone should give you some idea of just how tough it is to play quarterback.

Because the teams I've played on have had some degree of success, people who've never played football want to know how I went about my business. They'd like to see how I approached my craft, then apply that to their own. I think they'll find that the running themes throughout this book are commitment, preparation, and teamwork—and that these apply to more than just football.

Finally, this book is called *The Art and Magic of Quarterbacking*, because there's no secret scientific formula to help you play the position. Yes, there are fundamentals to taking a snap, dropping back to pass, and delivering the ball. Without having those down, you're going to struggle. But it's also about knowing your coaches' game plan, recognizing the opposition's strengths and weaknesses, and trusting your teammates. And it's about believing in yourself.

There's more to being a quarterback than arm strength, athletic ability, physical stature, and a booming voice. From practice and hard work come instincts. From instincts come art—and, on the best days, if you're fortunate, some magic.

—Joe Montana

Joe Montana's
Art and Magic
of Quarterbacking

FOOTBALL 101

George Will, pundit and avid baseball fan, once said, "Football combines the two worst things about America: it is violence punctuated by committee meetings." Mr. Will is entitled to his opinion, but I don't think he fully grasps what football is really all about. In competitive situations, things can get rough, even in his favorite sport—baseball. I can't recall the benches ever emptying in football—and certainly not because someone got hit with a ball.

MY SPORT

Well, there are several reasons why I think football is the best team sport going—teamwork, commitment, and innovation to name just three. But you know what? Too often you hear these very things used to criticize the sport.

Teamwork

In my opinion, there is no sport where you are more dependent on your teammates than football.

In basketball, one man can take over a game. In fact, in the pros they outlawed the zone defense specifically so that could happen. When Michael Jordan is isolated against his defender and he sticks a jumper, you're seeing something you'll never see in a football game—a man scoring all by himself. That doesn't mean it isn't tough to do or fun to watch, and it doesn't mean that basketball isn't a team sport; at its best, that's exactly what it is. I played point guard on a championship team in high school. My intramural team in college beat a team that had future NBA star Kelly Tripucka on it. I know what can happen when five guys play with one purpose in mind. I love basketball, and if it wasn't for my back, I'd still be playing it.

You have to rely so much more on your teammates in football. One great player can come out of college and turn a

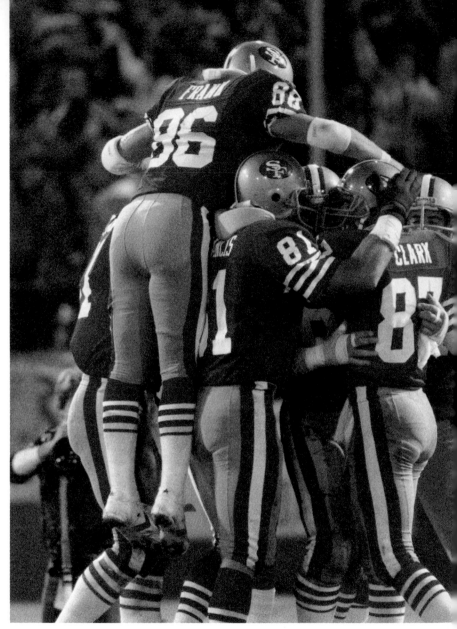

Each player must carry out his individual responsibility in order for the offensive unit to succeed. Joe says that individual players on defense can make their unit succeed.

basketball franchise from a doormat to a playoff team overnight. That doesn't happen very often in football.

In baseball, most of the players on the field do very little on any given pitch. When the ball is hit, chances are good that only two or three players will be involved in the play.

It Takes 11 to Win

In 1965, the Chicago Bears drafted two of the greatest players in history: Gale Sayers and Dick Butkus. They played together for five full seasons, but never made the playoffs. Their teams went 29-38-3. Ten years later, the 4-10 Bears drafted another all-time great: Walter Payton. They went 4-10 again, and it took them 3 years to get to the playoffs and 11 to win a championship.

Archie Manning, father of Tennessee State's Peyton Manning, was a great quarterback who happened to play for really bad teams—so bad, in fact, that in 13 NFL seasons his teams went 47-139-3 and never had a winning record. He was the second overall pick in the 1971 draft (behind Jim Plunkett, another quarter-back who struggled with bad teams), and his name can be found with the all-time leaders in completions, completion percentage, yards passing, touchdowns, inter-ception percent-age, you name it—but Archie Manning couldn't turn the New Orleans Saints into winners all by himself.

Unless you are the pitcher or catcher, it's tough to stay involved all the time. We can see this with my kids now: If the ball doesn't come to them, they're out there picking weeds and throwing stuff at rabbits. Just like I did.

In football, one man missing an assignment can be the difference between success or failure of the play. To win, everyone has to contribute. I get too much credit for engi-neering the drive that beat the Bengals in Super Bowl XXIII. No one talks about the protection I received or the patterns that were run or the plays that were called by Bill Walsh. I did not take over that game; our entire offensive unit did.

Commitment

I hear people telling me how they won't let their kid play football because it's too dangerous. It's a tough sport, and accidents do happen. If a kid isn't committed to playing well—or worse, if he's being pushed into it by an overzealous parent—maybe he's better off skipping it. But I say if a kid really wants to play, let him play. He's more likely to get hurt in a pickup game without pads or helmets than he is in an organized game with the proper protective equipment. More importantly, if a kid really wants to do well at football and is willing to make the necessary sacrifices, he will gain a whole

Bill Walsh built a dynasty during the 1980s in San Francisco. His famous West Coast Offense picked apart NFL defenses and helped lead the 49ers to three Super Bowls during his reign as head coach.

lot of valuable skills as a result—physical, mental, and emotional.

He'll need to be in good physical condition and will have to make some sacrifices to get there. He'll need to be prepared to do repetitive drills to address the weaknesses in his game. He'll need to be willing to make the mental commitment to learn the plays and analyze the opposition's strengths and weaknesses. Finally, he'll learn to handle adversity—to take a hit and get back up, to adjust when things don't work the way they were drawn up, and to know what it feels like to do his part to help a team win.

Everyone has to deal with adversity at some point. If a kid can experience it during a football game and figure out how to handle it, he'll be that much better off when he has to face it when it really matters.

Innovation

Some people criticize football because of how complicated it is. Now try to imagine these same folks using that logic to argue for checkers over chess. Football is complicated. No apologies. It's complicated because the sport allows—in fact, it demands—innovation. Stop thinking, start losing.

Baseball has evolved less than any other sport, because the sport doesn't really call for it. The game still boils down to pitcher versus hitter, and it's a lot easier for a coach to get creative with 11 players than it is with just one. Because the offense in baseball hasn't done all that much to change how it scores, the defense hasn't had to do much to keep up except come up with a new pitch every 10 years. That's why the defensive players are all standing where they've always been. Maybe an opposing manager thought about putting his right fielder in the bleachers back in the '20s when Babe Ruth started hitting home runs—but that's against the rules.

Football players today, on either side of the ball, are too big, too fast, too strong, and too athletic for the opposition to settle into predictable patterns and expect to succeed. If they do, they'll get chewed up. Most people think of football as only a game of brawn, but all teams have big strong players. A losing team will still look good going through the airport. Because of that, it's often the brains that are the difference

Joe Montana shares a laugh with head coach Bill Walsh after defeating the Minnesota Vikings to earn a trip to the NFC championship game in 1989. Bill Walsh was a brilliant innovator and Montana proved to be the perfect player to help him implement those ideas.

between winning and losing. Every defense can be exploited, if the offensive unit can execute these innovations.

Consider the pace of change in the NFL, where it's been a game of cat-and-mouse between offense and defense since the very beginning. This has stimulated some of the best football minds in history to come up with dramatically different ways to succeed. (See *120 Years of Football in 10 Minutes* on page 206.)

MY POSITION

Looking back on it, I wanted to be a quarterback right away. I didn't always get to play the position, though. They tried me at running back first. At the Pop Warner level, I'd get in when

Dan Marino , like Joe Montana, are just part of a long line of great NFL quarterbacks who came out of Western Pennsylvania.

somebody else got hurt. I kind of liked being a wide receiver, but I never got to play that much either. In high school, they even tried to make me a defensive back. A coach put me in at safety during an All-Star game, because he wanted me to play both offense and defense. I tried to suggest to him what a huge mistake this was going to be, but he found out soon enough. I took a couple of steps with the receiver I was supposed to be covering, then said, "Oh, was *that* my guy?" They moved me back to quarterback to keep the scoring down.

Other than an inability to cover wide receivers, I look for seven things in a quarterback. In addition to the physical skills, I look for mental skills, drive, leadership, resourcefulness, courage, and a respect for the game.

Mental Skills

In addition to the physical aspects, I want to know about the mental side of his game. This involves both being able to master the game plan and being strong enough emotionally to cope with the chaotic environment where that game plan gets implemented. He'll need to be able to read defenses, handle pressure, and maintain poise. He'll need to be able to think like a coach—both his own team's *and* his opposition's—so he can anticipate what will be done to try to stop him. He'll need to have unflagging confidence, not just in his own abilities, but in those of his teammates.

The mental aspect of sports is underappreciated, but I believe it's what truly separates Michael Jordan from the rest of the planet. The same goes for hockey's Wayne Gretzky, who was never the biggest, strongest, or fastest guy on his team. The mental part of the game is the toughest, and it's the reason so many rookies struggle. Coming out of college before graduation and having to make the adjustment to the pro game a year or two early just makes it that much more difficult. Underclassmen couldn't go pro when I was in college. That wouldn't have mattered for me, anyway. I didn't have to worry about the temptation of coming out before my senior year at Notre Dame—I'd been there for four years, but I'd only been a starter for one!

Drive

In addition to mental toughness, I want to see a competitive drive—a determination to get the most out of himself, to understand his role, and to be willing to put in the time in the film room, in the weight room, and on the practice field. You have to work extremely hard to succeed as a quarterback—not just because you need to know the game plan, be in excellent physical shape, and hone your skills, but because your teammates will be watching you to see how you go about your business. How you carry yourself will rub off on your teammates.

I came from a blue-collar, hard-working, tough-playing area, just one of many quarterbacks that the mining country of western Pennsylvania has produced. Johnny Unitas, Joe Namath, Daryle Lamonica, Jim Kelly, and Dan Marino are some others. I think if you go back and check the successful quarterbacks in the NFL, you'll find that very few came from privileged backgrounds. I read where Boomer Esiason said that one thing he had going for him was "not being born with a silver spoon in [his] mouth." There's a lot to be said for that. It's a nasty sport and, at quarterback, you're out there with a target on your chest. You've got to really have that hunger.

On quarterbacking: "It's the greatest job anybody could ever want. All the pressure, the excitement, the power, the fun, the struggle—it's all rolled up into one."

—*Boomer Esiason, quarterback*

Earning Their Stripes

Most rookie quarterbacks don't get to see much action. The coach wants them to look and learn, so he spares them the physical and mental abuse that complicated pro defenses can inflict on someone not used to seeing them. Bill Walsh broke Joe Montana in slowly as a rookie, letting him throw only 23 passes. When you consider how these all-time greats did when playing regularly as rookies in the NFL, you realize how mentally challenging the position really is.

	Pass Attempts	% Intercepted	% Completed	TD / Int
Troy Aikman	293	6%	53%	9 / 18
Terry Bradshaw	218	11%	38%	6 / 24
John Elway	259	5%	47%	7 / 14
Dan Fouts	194	7%	45%	6 / 13

Leadership

Someone who is driven, and who recognizes that his drive can inspire others, is on his way to being a leader. Some players want to be leaders but try to do too much. They think leadership is trying to take the team on their shoulders and win the game on their own. More than a few football players have tried to do it, but *I've* never seen anyone actually do it.

Everyone has their own style of leadership. Some guys are comfortable being the charismatic, swaggering field general who drives and intimidates "his men." I never approached things that way, never thought of it as "my team." I took a we're-all-in-this-together approach, which suited my personality. If my teammates made a mistake, I tried to help them rather than scream at them. That way, when I made a mistake, they were there to pick me up.

In many ways, leadership is simply the ability to bring out the best in your teammates. To do that, you have to understand their roles—*everyone's* roles—so you can figure out how to help put them in the best position to succeed. Some people don't want that responsibility, and that's fine. It's impossible to have any success as a quarterback, though, without being

> "To be honest, I thought I could do it all in one year. I really did. I didn't realize that in pro football you start from scratch. You have to relearn everything from the very beginning. It's a brand new ball game all the way."
>
> —*Terry Bradshaw*

a leader, since all eyes in the huddle will be on you. If you're uncertain about things, your teammates will know .

Resourcefulness

No one becomes a leader overnight. It's something that has to be earned, and the best way to do that is to have some success on the field—success not just when things are going well, but when it's not your day. That takes creativity, resourcefulness, and a refusal to accept that something can't be done. It's the ability to help your offensive unit make something out of nothing.

It doesn't hurt to have an active imagination, either—or a poker face. Jets fans won't appreciate me dredging up a bad memory, but Dan Marino helped put the Dolphins in first place late in the 1994 season with a pretty creative play. The Dolphins had come back from 24-6 to 24-21 and were running a two-minute drill late in the 4th quarter. With the clock running and the ball in close, Dan ran up to the line of scrimmage, signaling to his teammates that he was going to spike the ball and stop the clock. He was signaling to the Jets' defense, too, though. The Jets relaxed and, after taking the snap, Dan took one step and fired a touchdown strike into the corner of the end zone instead. The Dolphins won 28-24 and went on to take the division, while the Jets lost 32 of their next 36 games.

Courage

Being a quarterback is also about courage. It takes guts to step on the playing field, whatever position you play. It's not just quarterbacks who are vulnerable. You can get crushed fielding a punt, busting a wedge on a kick return, or going over the middle as a receiver. Dropping back to pass with a blitzing linebacker coming at you on the blindside, stepping up in the pocket when the outside pressure heats up, delivering a pass knowing that you're about to get buried—it's not easy, but it has to be done. Your teammates expect it from you. When you come through, you've earned the right to expect the same from them. Sure, it's safer on the sidelines, but as I said during my last two years in San Francisco, if you're comfortable there you'll stay there.

"One of the things I love about football is that you have the full run of emotions and pressures. In fact, every chance I get to talk to any young man, I encourage him to get into athletics, football in particular. It shows you yourself. You must function under pressure. . . . A person either faces up to what it takes . . . or he runs away. Anyone who keeps running is in for a life of misery."

—Chuck Noll

GUTS

Consider the frustrations that New York Giants quarterback Phil Simms endured without giving in. When he was drafted in the first round in 1979 as an unknown out of tiny Morehead State, Giants fans wailed in dismay. As a rookie in 1979, he looked good in a half-season of work. Then in 1980 he separated his shoulder. He separated it again in 1981, missing the playoffs. He missed the entire 1982 season with a knee injury. Then in 1983, he missed 14 games when he fractured his thumb on a helmet during the follow-through on one of his passes. No one could have blamed him if he just tossed in his cards and went home to Kentucky, but over the next three seasons, he led the Giants to three playoff appearances, culminating in a near-flawless performance in a Super Bowl XXI victory over Denver.

Phil Simms overcame a number of injuries early in his career to become one of the greatest players to ever suit up for the New York Giants. His courage was eventually rewarded, as he enjoyed one of the greatest games by a quarterback in Super Bowl history in January 1987.

Respect

Finally, a quarterback has to have a respect for the game—and that means teammates, coaches, *and* opponents. You can respect your opponent and still want to beat him. Just look at Larry Bird and Magic Johnson, who both acknowledge that their respect for one another helped them raise the level of their own games.

It's one thing to have a little fun talking trash to your opponents. It's another to get personal, or to do it to call attention to yourself. When I played, we all talked to each other. The fans didn't know because we were doing it for

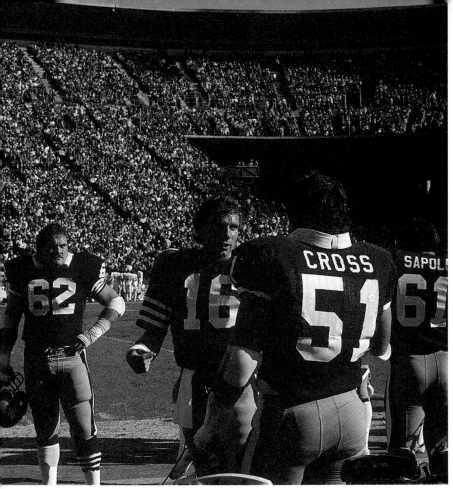

Montana believes that leadership is simply bringing out the best in your teammates. An integral part of that is listening to what they have to say.

laughs most of the time, not to pick fights, and we didn't pound our chests for the camera.

That's all part of knowing how to win as well as how to lose. I like to see quarterbacks who don't point fingers, who don't seek credit or duck blame, and who recognize that they're part of a team, not out there starring in their own movie.

Physical Skills

Now that we've covered what they call the "intangibles"—and, believe me, if *they* spent more time in huddles with guys like Namath and Bradshaw, *they* would realize these things are *very* tangible—we can move on to the physical aspects.

RESOURCEFULNESS

Probably the best example of creativity on the football field in recent memory came in September 1978. The Raiders were down 20-14 with ten seconds to go and the ball at the Chargers' 14-yard line. Raiders quarterback Ken Stabler was about to be sacked to end the game. "The Snake" had been finding ways to pass his team to come-from-behind wins his entire career, but this time a fumble was in order. He rolled the ball toward the end zone, and two more Raiders batted the ball forward, with tight end Dave Casper falling on it for the game-winning touchdown. It was so creative that the NFL decided that it should be illegal. The touchdown stood, but during the offseason, the league rules committee decided that a fumble on fourth down or during the final two minutes of a half could only be advanced by the man who fumbled.

Montana unleashes a sideline pass for a short gain at the Houston Astrodome. Passes of five to 10 yards were a trademark of Montana and the 49ers' offense.

It would be easy enough to say that the ideal quarterback should be built like Drew Beldsoe, with the accuracy of Dan Marino and the running ability of Steve Young. A bit more on the subject should be said, though. Let's take each of those physical attributes in turn.

Size

There is a lot of talk about size when people scout quarter-backs coming out of college. A quarterback needs to be tall enough to see over the offensive line and big enough to take a hit from the defensive line—and as these linemen have gotten bigger, so too have the quarterbacks. Back in 1960, when there were very few 300-pounders in the NFL, the Cowboys quarterback during their first year of existence was 5'9" Eddie LeBaron. Few quarterbacks were more than 200 pounds. Today, quarterbacks have started to look more like linebackers—Brett Favre is 6'2" 220 pounds, Troy Aikman is 6'4" 230, and Drew Bledsoe is 6'5" 235. These guys are the same size as Ray Nitschke and bigger than Jack Lambert. I'm 6'2" 200 pounds, which is relatively small.

I think the size thing is a bit overemphasized. The Eagles made it to the playoffs in 1996 with a pair of 6' quarter-backs, Rodney Peete and Ty Detmer. Mark Bruncll is 6'1" and he has established himself as a star. The best example, though, is 6' Jeff Blake of the Bengals, who the Jets never really gave a chance—and they've been regretting it ever since. You can find plenty of tall quarterbacks who throw too many interceptions, and big quarterbacks who can't take hits.

Accuracy

For me, there are other, much more important physical attributes than height and weight, namely the ability to throw a football accurately. The importance of being able to throw the ball 70 yards in the air is overrated, especially in today's passing game where timing and precision are so much more critical. It's not as if you have to throw the ball that far on every play. Next time you're watching a game, count how many times a ball is thrown more than 45 yards (a distance that just about anyone can learn to reach). It won't be many. In fact, during my first few years with the 49ers, we practiced on a small field with only about 50 yards of grass, so you couldn't throw it farther than that anyway. There are different ways to get the ball where you want it go. As long as you're smart about execution, everything else will fall into place. It didn't bother me a bit to throw ten yards to Jerry Rice and let him run 65. Six points is six points.

ACCURACY

Bernie Kosar was a very underrated quarterback, who didn't look particu-larly smooth in the pocket and was probably one of the slowest players in the NFL. He was smart, though, and he was accurate, and he simply did not throw intercep-tions. In fact, he's the best all-time at that—2.5%, just ahead of Joe Montana at 2.6%. His accuracy was one of the reasons he was able to guide his team to the playoffs his first five seasons in the league. Not even Dan Marino—who was great in the NFL from day one, top ranked in the AFC *as a rookie!*—was able to match that. Kosar's Cleveland Browns teams were 49-29-1 from 1985 through 1989 and, if not for John Elway, might have been in three Super Bowls instead of the Denver Broncos.

Here's another thing about accuracy over brute strength: most defensive players will tell you that they hate being scored on no matter how you do it, but they'd rather get burned for one big play than have an offense march down the field on a 15-play drive. If they give up the big play, it might very well be because of one player and one missed assignment. It's a lot tougher to maintain your confidence when an offense has just spent the last ten minutes pushing the ball down your throat.

Mobility

When most fans think of quarterbacks, they think arms, but without the legs and feet, a quarterback won't be getting many opportunities to show off his arm. Besides, there's a lot more to legs and feet than just scrambling. Dan Marino isn't known for his speed or his running ability, but he has very quick feet, which helps him get set up in the pocket that much faster and gives him that much longer to read the defense. That, and his incredibly quick release, kept him from taking too many hits. Another quarterback without foot speed, Dan Fouts, could get set up quicker by backpedaling than some quarterbacks who use the "faster" crossover drop we'll be discussing later.

Joe Namath had very nimble feet, too, before he blew out his knees. Namath was known for throwing deep, but when he still had his wheels, I think he would have been great in Bill Walsh's possession-passing offense. The 49ers' system calls for a lot of sprint-out passes—that's what I threw to Dwight Clark in the championship against the Cowboys—and without those quick feet, the play will take too long to develop and the timing just won't work.

Bill Walsh told me that my footwork was what he liked most about me when he worked me out prior to the 1979 draft. Maybe that's why he said that at my first training camp I looked like a Swedish placekicker.

RELENTLESS

A fierce pass rush can make for a long afternoon for a quarterback—or a short one, if he's knocked out of the game. Seattle quarterback Dave Krieg was put on the ground nine times by the Chiefs—an NFL record seven times by linebacker Derrick Thomas—during a game in Kansas City in November 1990. He kept getting back up, though, and the Seahawks were down only 16-10 with four seconds to go and the ball on the Kansas City 25-yard line. Thomas had Krieg in his arms for number eight, but the quarterback wriggled free and threw a game-winning touchdown pass on the last play of the game.

Not Your Average Joes

Broadway Joe and Joe Montana both came out of western Pennsylvania and are the only two players to quarterback a championship team in both the NCAA and NFL. As pros they played under very different systems, though. In his prime, Namath played in the AFL, where teams threw deep and often to stretch the defense. Quarterbacks racked up a lot of yardage—and a lot of incompletions and interceptions. During the Jets' Super Bowl season, Namath completed less than 50% of his passes and threw more interceptions than touchdowns—and was still the third-ranked quarterback in the league! That's because he averaged nearly 17 yards a completion! (In his career, Montana completed more than 63% of his passes, threw nearly twice as many touchdowns than interceptions—but averaged "only" 12 yards a completion.)

In the late-'60s, this "mad bomber" style of play was considered inferior by the established NFL—and the Jets went into Super Bowl III against the Baltimore Colts as 18-point underdogs. Most fans know that Namath guaranteed a victory and delivered it, 16-7. How did the Jets do it? Running the ball the NFL way? Not really. They ran a bit more than they did during the regular season—43 rushes compared to a season average of 33—but they still gained less than 3.5 yards per attempt. No, the big adjustment was in Namath's approach to passing. The Colts blitzed frequently, but he was only sacked twice and threw no interceptions. He dumped the ball off rather than take the loss, and he didn't hurry any throws into coverage. He played a possession passing game. The results looked very Montana-like:

	Att	Comp	% Comp	Yards	Yd/Comp	TD	Int	Sacks
Namath Super Bowl III	28	17	61%	206	12	0	0	2
Montana Super Bowl XVI	22	14	64%	157	11	1	0	1

GETTING IT STARTED

As I've already said, the quarterback's arm is not the most important aspect of his game. Here we'll cover the fundamentals of starting the play and getting into position to pass—all of which are vital and none of which involve throwing the football: taking the snap, handing off the ball, and dropping into the pocket. We'll also cover some plays that require you to be a good actor as you drop back from center: draw plays and play-action passes.

But first things first . . .

EQUIPMENT

You need to make certain that you have the proper protective equipment. Now, you might be wondering how you're supposed to relax and concentrate when you're strapping on 15 pounds of war gear. Like anything else, you just have to get used to it over time. Even though I was one of the smallest guys out there and playing one of the most vulnerable positions, I tried to wear as little equipment as possible. I figured my mobility was my best defense. Think about it. A quarterback who dressed himself in a suit of armor would get killed out there. That doesn't mean you should go out there without any padding, but it does mean you shouldn't be so intent on protecting every square of inch of your body that you can't execute.

For example, I kept wearing the smallest shoulder pads even though other quarterbacks were beginning to wear the same ones as the position players. Shoulder pads are made for hitting and protecting a blow coming from the top of your shoulder. A quarterback rarely, if ever, gets hit like that. You get hit in the back portion of your shoulder pads or in the chest plate. Meanwhile, the heavy protection on your shoulders may restrict your throwing. Put a little more padding in the chest or in the back, but keep the arms free. I

> "You've got to be so strong mentally to make it. As soon as the ball is snapped, the violence and the sheer noise . . . makes it so hard to make an intelligent, quick decision."
>
> —Mike Holmgren, Green Bay Packers head coach and former USC quarterback

Montana kept his equipment to a minimum to maintain his mobility whenever possible. Here he's shown wearing extra protection around his rib cage, which can take a beating at the quarterback position.

didn't like to wear anything on my arms. Just a ¾-length shirt. After my elbow surgery, they made me wear an elastic brace, but I got used to that fairly quickly.

There are plenty of helmets for a quarterback to choose from, but, again, the heavier ones are not necessarily better. Helmets were designed to protect ball-carriers and tacklers against head-to-head hits, but quarterbacks rarely get hit that way. Find a helmet that feels right and don't worry so much about the weight. As for the facemask, quarterbacks used to wear the thinnest ones on the field except for the kickers. Now everyone seems to be protecting their faces more—that's fine, just as long as you can see the field . . .

I didn't wear a mouth piece for awhile, and I regretted it when dentists had to perform two root canals because of cracked teeth. Teams provide mouthpieces that allow a quarterback to call out signals, and they claim that you can talk normally while wearing one—emphasis on the word *claim*. Wear one and get used to it.

Like the shoulder pads, quarterbacks also strip down their leg pads. Again, most quarterbacks don't get hit down there, unless it's an accident. Guys want to have their legs free, as if they're in shorts, so they can move. I rarely taped my ankles for practice but usually had them done for games. It was good support. They tried to get me to wear knee braces at one point, but that didn't work. Too restrictive. I liked my shoes to fit like a glove, so I wore them as tight as possible. I wore size 10½ my entire playing career and I only found out recently that I really have a size 12 foot. I guess I figured that if my shoes were so tight that it hurt, I wasn't going to slip in them. Go with whatever works.

TAKING THE SNAP

Now that we're suited up, let's get started. Everything begins with the snap. The center is a position that many people, including quarterbacks, take for granted. But you only have about three seconds to decide what is happening downfield, to follow the routes, and to figure out what you should be doing with the ball. You don't want to waste any time thinking, "I've got to get the snap right."

You need to get to the point where you're not even thinking about the snap. It's trickier than it looks on television, so repetitions are vital. For one thing, you'll never see the transfer of the ball from the center to you. Your head will be up, watching the defense. For another, you'll be taking snaps from more than one center during the course of the season, so you need to work with the first two or three guys on the depth chart during preseason. Try to get comfortable with each. The height of the center will determine how much you need to bend your knees, where you put your hands, and

The throwing hand should be under center, palm down. Your other hand should have the palm facing slightly forward. Your thumbs should be connected forming a pocket. Flex your elbows slightly to absorb the force of the snap.

how close you stand to him. Some centers will snap the ball a little more forward, some a little farther back. If you don't adjust, the snap will be muffed.

Work with these different centers and get comfortable with your stance. You'll be turning and pivoting in all sorts of directions once you get the ball, depending on the play that's been called, so good balance is critical. Some quarterbacks change slightly how they plant their feet depending on the type of play that has been called—a sprint-out to the right, for instance, compared to a handoff to the left. It can help you get away from center more quickly, but this is a good idea *only* if you can get away with it. Don't be too obvious about your footwork, because that can tip off the defense about what play is coming.

The problem for some quarterbacks isn't tipping off the defense by cheating a bit to get away from center more quickly—it's losing valuable seconds and messing up the timing of certain plays by getting away too *slowly*. Sometimes it's a matter of taking two steps to get away from the line instead of just one step, because the quarterback has to reposition one foot before he can move away from the line with the other. If you're finding yourself doing this—instead of pivoting smoothly—you'll need to experiment with your stance until you can get away from center more cleanly. One thing you might try is turning your feet inward slightly. That has helped a number of quarterbacks.

Footwork is obviously important, but if you don't hold your hands correctly it won't matter, because the ball will end up on the ground. A lot of fans assume that the ball is coming back point-first, and that the quarterback has both hands under center to take it. Well, most centers deliver the ball with a quarter-turn. That means it will be delivered to you with the seams parallel to the line of scrimmage. To take that kind of snap, you need to have your throwing hand under center, palm down, and the other next to it, palm forward. You spread your fingers each about an inch apart and hold your hands together at the thumbs so that your palms form a pocket for the ball. Your elbows should be slightly bent—but not so much that you won't be able to absorb the force of the snap. Use your top hand to put some pressure on the center's butt, letting let him know where you want the ball. Too much

A Shotgun Start

Back in the 1920s of the NFL, when the single-wing was the most common formation, the long snap or "shotgun" was the standard way for the center to deliver the ball and start the play. Only it wasn't called the shotgun, the ball was being snapped to the fullback, and teams rarely threw out of it.

The Dallas Cowboys resurrected this approach in the mid-70s, having Roger Staubach stand five yards behind the center in obvious passing situations. Many NFL teams eventually added this formation to their offense, some placing a lone setback near the quarterback so that the defense had to respect the possibility of a run.

In the shotgun, the quarterback begins to side-step another five yards once the ball hits his hands. Some quarterbacks don't like it, because they feel that looking for the football takes their eyes off of the defense. Others swear by it, because it enables them to get a deep drop more quickly and allows them to survey the defense at the snap of the ball.

The 49ers ran it exactly twice. On the first, they completed a pass for ten yards. On the second, the ball was snapped about ten yards over Joe Montana's head, and Bill Walsh had seen enough.

pressure, though, will push your hands apart and that's going to mean a fumble.

In this position, the ball will be hitting your throwing hand, and your opposite hand will instinctively close on it. If the center has positioned the ball correctly, the seams should be hitting your fingers, so you should be able to get your proper throwing grip on the ball quickly. Keep both hands on the ball until you're ready to deliver it—either on a handoff or a pass. When you're younger and your hands are small, this is a matter of necessity. Whatever the age, most quarterback fumbles happen because there's only one hand on the ball. Sometimes your own guy—a pulling guard, perhaps—can knock it loose. Often, it's an outside rusher stripping it.

Finally, I have one other word of advice on taking the snap. Make certain that you don't line up under one of your guards. I did that once in high school. Let's just say that this formation won't revolutionize offense as we know it.

HANDING OFF THE BALL

There are basically four types of handoffs: the *front, under-neath, reverse-pivot*, and *toss*. Regardless of the type of handoff, you should be coming away from center with both hands on the ball, and the ball tucked into your stomach. You should be getting out quickly, so that you can get the ball to the running back as deep in the backfield as possible—and so that a guard won't step on your foot. You see quarterbacks tripping now and then when they drop back from center. Most of the time that's the quarterback's fault for not being quick enough on his drop.

On fronts, underneaths, and reverse-pivots, your running back may want the ball in his hands or his stomach (left elbow up, right arm underneath if he's on your right, the opposite if he's on your left). Either way, you need to be delivering the ball not just with your hand but with your eyes, so that you're certain he's got it. And you need to be continuing to drop into the backfield after the ball is handed off, so you won't make it easy for the defense to tell whether it's a run or a pass. This is important, because when you do fake a handoff for a play-action pass, you want to look just like you do after a real handoff.

Front

Say you're sending your tailback off left tackle out of an I-formation, and you're using a front handoff. Your first step is with your left foot to the left. The angle of this first step depends on the type of run and the formation—in this instance, it will be close to 45 degrees (almost like the sprint-out, which we'll be discussing later in this chapter). On a quicker hitting play—say a dive play where the ball-carrier is lined up closer to the line of scrimmage—you'd be stepping almost parallel to the line of scrimmage.

After you step with your left, you take a cross-over step with your right. As you step again with your left, you're extending the ball in your right hand and preparing to stick it into your runner's stomach. As you deliver the ball, your feet are even—which means that you've taken two-and-a-half steps from the center. At the handoff, you are between the

Carry the ball with two hands and locate your target with both eyes. Here Joe executes a front handoff on the practice field.

ball-carrier and the line of scrimmage. The front is the quickest handoff a quarterback will make, and it is designed more for speed than deception.

Underneath

On the underneath handoff, the transfer will take place with the ball-carrier between you and the line. Your first step will look like a front handoff, but your next will be straight back, rather than diagonal to the line of scrimmage. You will end up crossing the ball-carrier's path before handing him the ball.

You use the underneath handoff on traps and counters—misdirection plays where the runner is trying to get the defense thinking that a play is going another way, usually by

Montana turns to deliver a front handoff during Super Bowl XIX. He's got both hands on the ball, and he's holding it close to his body, taking good care of the package before he delivers it.

taking his first step in the opposite direction. You're doing your part to misdirect the defense by stepping with your right foot to the right on runs to the *left* (and vice versa).

Reverse-Pivot

The reverse-pivot is the toughest handoff you can make. The quarterback has to turn 270 degrees before handing off the ball—and do so fairly quickly. You'll end up handing off the ball in the identical position as you do on a front, but rather than turning in the direction of the play you turn your back

A Gigantic Fumble

On November 19, 1978, the Giants had a 17-12 lead over the Eagles and were running out the clock in the game's final minute. Then an assistant coach called for a reverse-pivot handoff that would cost him his job. Larry Csonka and quarterback Joe Pisarcik muffed the transfer. Eagles defensive back Herman Edwards scooped up the ball and ran it in for the winning touchdown. In the media firestorm after the game, fans in the New York area were given an education about the different types of handoffs—which only served to further fuel the controversy. If you use this type of handoff to confuse the defense, why call for it in the final minute of a game when you're running out the clock? Why not just take a knee? And if you were going to run it, why not a front handoff that was a lot easier to execute?

Three years later, the Giants would have Phil Simms and Lawrence Taylor on their roster and their first trip to the playoffs in 18 years. They would go on to win Super Bowls XXI and XXV—with no fumbles in either victory.

Meanwhile, Giants head coach John McVay had moved on to the 49ers organization—where he helped convince the team to use a third-round draft pick in 1979 on a guy named Joe Montana.

---

to the line of scrimmage and "take the long way." On plays to the right, your first move from center is a pivot on your right foot followed by a long stride with your left that takes you to the delivery point.

This leads to yet another reason why you need to have both hands on the ball until you're ready to hand it off. A front handoff to the right and a reverse-pivot handoff to the left all start identically—with the quarterback turning to the right. Say you've developed the bad habit of carrying the ball in one hand too early in the play. Well, that would mean that on the front handoff to the right, the ball would be in your *left* hand—and on a reverse-pivot handoff to the left the ball would be in your *right* hand. So much for mixing up the defense. At any level where films are being studied, that will be picked up, and you could tip off where the play is going on your very first movement.

> "We never stop working on the fundamentals—drops, protection pockets, where to go when the pocket breaks. We don't leave all that stuff in training camp."
>
> —Joe Montana, 1981

Montana executes an underneath handoff to teammate Wendell Tyler. Notice that Roger Craig (33) is also doing his part to make the defense think the play is going to the left.

And there's no point in executing a relatively tricky handoff like this if the defense isn't going to be fooled.

Toss

With a toss or pitch-out, you can throw the ball with a spiral or end-over-end. The spiral requires more complicated footwork, so I would suggest the end-over-end. When tossing end over end, the ball is held with two hands, out in front of you and low to the ground, point down. You deliver it to the runner with the ball not even making a full revolution. More important than how you toss it, though, is that you are consistent about it, lead the runner, and hit him in the numbers. You don't want him to break stride or have to reach back to

"Got to have timing. It all starts with good drops."

—Sid Gillman, Hall of Fame coach and known as the founder of the modern passing game

get it. Remember, this isn't an incomplete pass if it hits the ground. It's a live ball. If you lead him properly, he'll be going full-speed when he catches it and will be able to have his shoulders square to the line of scrimmage as he heads upfield. Just as backs want handoff deep in the backfield, they want their tosses as far outside as possible so they can get wide quickly.

A toss may be run with either front or reverse-pivot footwork, though you can pitch it farther on the latter because you have more momentum. Either way, turn 45 degrees to the line of scrimmage, and follow through as the ball leaves your hand, just like a pass. This will improve your accuracy.

DROPPING INTO THE POCKET

In San Francisco, we were able to play a possession game by throwing the football to set up the run. To make that work, we had to be quick and in rhythm. Without proper footwork on your drop, you'll find it very hard to get into that good rhythm.

There are two basic ways to drop: crossover and back-pedal. The backpedal, which Dan Fouts used with amazing results, allows you to see the field with both eyes as you drop, and eliminates your blindside—but it's slower. It's also harder to get your weight going forward again, although Dan was enough of an arm-thrower that he could overcome that. Almost all quarterbacks use the crossover, which is the one we'll be covering, because it allows you to get set up more quickly.

Regardless of how you choose to get back into the pocket, there are four basic drops: 3-step, 5-step, 7-step, and sprint-out. The footwork is different on each, but some things remain constant.

- You need to keep both hands on the ball with the point "pointing" to the ground.

- You need to hold it close to your body with both elbows tucked in, or you're inviting a strip.

Joe shows an example of a three-step drop. Notice how he pushes hard off his left leg to get full extension in the first step. Montana crosses over with his left leg and halts momentum with his right leg to set up to pass. Notice throughout his drop Montana stays on the balls of his feet to maintain stability. This drop is used primarily for quick outs and slants which San Francisco used frequently.

- Front-hand pressure on the ball will push it into throwing position when you stop your drop—and make it more difficult to be stripped.

- Holding the ball near your chest rather than your stomach near the end of your drop will have the same benefits as front-hand pressure.

Those "little things" can add up to a quicker release.

Amazingly, some teams—even at the pro level—don't teach much footwork. Moreover, some teams don't even have set footwork. They let the quarterbacks pick it. They just don't worry about it that much because they don't have a rhythmic passing attack.

3-Step Drop

The 3-step drop is used for *slants* and *quick* outs—short patterns that are covered in detail in Chapter 3. If you're right-handed, you will pivot on your left foot so that your shoulders are parallel to the sideline, while stepping back with your right foot. You cross over with your left foot, then land and plant on the inside ball of your right foot. Don't land too flat-footed, or it will throw off your balance. As you land and plant on your right foot, use your front hand to push your right hand into throwing position. If your primary receiver is on the right, try to land with your heel turned toward the line of scrimmage, which will shift your weight toward your target. If your primary receiver is on the left, try to land with your toes turned toward the line of scrimmage for the same reason. Work on this until all wasted motion has been eliminated, since you really want this to be *four* steps: step, cross, plant, throw.

The 3-step passes were vital to our possession passing game in San Francisco. These are the "long handoffs" or "dinks and dunks" people sometimes talk about when they describe the West Coast Offense. Because these plays were designed to develop so quickly, timing was more critical on these passes than any others. And that meant setting up in the pocket as quickly as possible.

There is another very good reason why the quarterback needs to set up quickly on these plays. The toughest part of

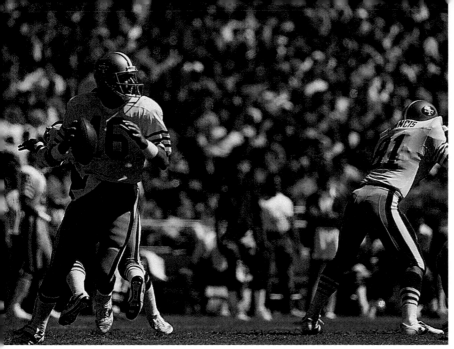

A deeper drop by the quarterback will allow more time for the play to develop and for receivers to run longer routes downfield. Notice how Montana plants on his back leg. He's now in position to shift his weight forward and throw the ball with velocity.

the 3-step drop is that you're always close to the line after making those three steps. That means you're closer to the defenders—about four yards from them, in fact. Hold onto the ball too long and it will get batted down—since the short, quick passes are the flattest you'll throw.

Next time you watch an NFL game, check how many times a quarterback takes a 3-step drop and then count his completions. This should be a very high percentage pass. Try to notice if the incompletions are due to a bad throw or good coverage. Also notice how often he takes a 3-step drop, then has to stand in the pocket looking for a receiver. If the defense can consistently take away the primary receiver on this pass and force the offense out of its rhythm, then it could be a long day for that quarterback.

5-Step Drop

A 5-step drop is used for medium-range passes, including one of the toughest throws a quarterback has to make—the 10-to-15 yard *out*. This is the pattern where the receiver goes down

10 or 15 yards, then makes a right-angle turn toward the sidelines. This pass may only look like it's going 15 yards, but don't forget the distance from the pocket to the sideline. To cover half a football field *and* make it 15 yards downfield, you'll have to throw that ball 30 yards in the air. This is the one you see intercepted and returned for touchdowns if the quarterback does not have enough on the throw or has telegraphed his pass by staring down the receiver. It's much more important to be able to deliver this pass on a line than it is to heave one 60 yards in the air.

The mechanics for a 5-step drop are similar to the 3-step: pivot away from center, then step, cross, step, cross, plant, throw. We had two versions of a 5-step drop, one which included a hitch—a short step forward with your plant foot. You didn't deliver the ball as quickly with this extra hitch, but it did help you get a little more zip on the ball.

7-Step Drop

The 7-step drop is used for deeper patterns. Quarterbacks who like to throw deep certainly love this drop, but so do pass rushers. At least with the 7-step drop, which takes you about ten yards deep, you will be able to step farther up in the pocket if you start to feel some outside pressure.

The first half of the 7-step drop is identical to the 5-step drop: pivot then step, cross, step, cross. But rather than have two more long strides that make for a full head of steam as you try to plant, your final three steps are shorter with your body leaning slightly forward. Then, since you're often throwing deep out of this drop, you may need to gear up for it with a hitch. Even John Elway, who may have the strongest arm in football, sometimes takes this extra step forward—not unlike an outfielder's "crow hop" in baseball, but less pronounced.

Some quarterbacks will try to get deeper faster in a 7-step drop by turning their back to the line of scrimmage and sprinting back with their first three or four steps. They then bring themselves back under control and look downfield on their final steps. It's a trade-off—a quicker drop, but harder to read the defense.

Sprint-Out

This is not to be confused with scrambling. A sprint-out is planned, and it involves three parts: 1) dropping back at an angle to the line of scrimmage; then 2) moving parallel to the line; and finally 3) moving toward your target.

If you're a right-hander moving to the right, you take a 5-step drop from center at a 45-degree angle from the line of scrimmage. Slow down a bit as you take another five strides parallel to the line. Now the tricky part: get yourself square to where you expect to deliver the ball and shorten your strides. When you do throw the ball, it will be with your right foot back—just like a regular pass—but it will be with a flick of the right wrist, without much shoulder rotation at all. For a proper follow-through, keep running after the ball.

If you're a right-hander moving to the left, you take a steeper angle back from the line of scrimmage. The only other important difference is that as you move toward the line after running parallel, you need to make more of an effort to open your hips and shoulders to face the target. The steeper angle you take back from center will help you get square to where you expect to deliver the ball.

Some people say that what I've just described is throwing off the wrong foot. Some righties start to throw when their right foot is forward, and then try to get their body through the other way. But you can't get as much on the ball this way. And sometimes you could use a little bit extra on the ball. You'll get more air on it the way I've described—although be careful not to lean back too far or you'll air mail it right over your receiver. Really, you've got to be able to throw in an instant if someone is open, which means being able to go off either foot.

I began using sprint-out passes in high school. There are a lot of benefits to using it. You're not going to be sacked for a big loss, because you should be moving toward the line of scrimmage by the time you face any rush. If you are a good running quarterback, that threat may keep the linebackers from dropping back into coverage. You're making the pass rush run farther to get to you, which may eventually take its toll.

Joe sprints out to the left running parallel to the line of scrimmage. Once he locates his target, the squares his shoulders to the receiver and unleashes the ball on the run. If you notice in Figure 4, Joe throws off his right foot. This is a very difficult way to throw the football, but Montana was able to master it, delivering the ball with pinpoint accuracy.

Joe rolls out to the right in a playoff game against the Minnesota Vikings in 1989. Once the quarterback leaves the pocket, it forces the linebackers and defensive backs to make a decision: stay with the man they're covering or go after the man with the ball.

On your part, it requires a lot of work and good timing, since you're throwing on the run and you have to get your feet right, then your body. If you don't have a real strong arm and you're always looking for a way to get more on the ball, this is a good way to throw. This pass will let your body do most of the work in delivering the ball. If you really want to watch someone throw the ball well on the run, find a run-and-shoot team or a videotape of one. Most of these quarterbacks had it down. They could do just about whatever they wanted and still get a lot on the ball.

Early development in sprinting out is good for any quarterback. There will be a lot of times when you're forced to move out of the pocket, so you must learn to throw on the run. Of course, there are many great quarterbacks who get away without moving a lot, such as Dan Marino and Troy Aikman. They also have the big offensive lines, quick releases, and the strong arms to pull this off.

For a few years in San Francisco, we also ran sprint-out passes where I would stop and get set after running parallel to the line of scrimmage, rather than moving toward the target. This gave me a clearer view of the secondary, bought me some time from the pass rush, and gave the defense one more thing to worry about—but we eventually dropped it because the linemen felt they never knew where I was going to set up.

DRAWS AND PLAY-ACTION

We've covered footwork on runs and passes. But football isn't just about timing—it's also about deception. Here's what you have to do on runs that you want to look like passes, and passes that you want to look like runs.

Draw

Draw plays are slow-developing runs that are designed to look like passing plays. You drop back from center as if you're setting up to pass, while your running back stays in as if he's pass blocking. If you "sell" this pass well enough, the defense will be very vulnerable to a run straight up the middle.

Not only will you probably have some draw plays in your game plan, chances are it will be an audible for you if you're staring at a heavy rush coming from the outside. But it won't do much good with a heavy inside rush, since your runner will just be heading into the teeth of it.

These may be the plays that a quarterback and running back need to work on, more than any others, in order to get the timing down. There are three common forms of draw plays, with the big difference being the position of the running back relative to the quarterback. There is a draw play where a quarterback hands the ball forward to a running back that has already passed him; one where the runner has started to move forward, but has not passed the quarterback yet; and another where the running back receives the ball while standing still and playing the part of a pass blocker.

Unlike regular handoffs, on draw plays you bring the ball *to* the runner rather than meeting him. All types of draws require that the quarterback convince the defense that he is indeed dropping back to pass—and that means looking downfield, not at the eventual ball-carrier. It also means continuing to do so even after the handoff.

We didn't run many draws in San Francisco, because Bill Walsh preferred quicker-hitting plays. The primary draw we ran had me handing the ball forward to a runner I'd already passed on my fifth step—since many teams had tried to stop our short passing game by having their linebackers hold their spots until I'd taken the fourth step of my drop.

Play-Action

Play-action passes are the opposite of draw plays—passing plays designed to look like runs. Play-action passing is not hard to do, if you're willing to work at it and sweat the details. Boomer Esiason, who we faced in Super Bowl XXIII, was one of the best I've ever seen at it, and it had a *lot* to do with how far the Bengals went that year.

First of all, you can't just go through the motions. You can't just stick an empty hand in a runner's stomach while holding the ball in your throwing hand for all to see. You need to perform the identical motions that you would ordinarily make on a regular running play—including what you do *after* the handoff. Here is where the attention to detail can pay off. A few quarterbacks have had some success hiding the ball on their hip after the "handoff" on a play-action pass; if you want this to be even more effective, always include the hip move into your movements after a *real* handoff.

Of course, this approach requires big hands because you'll be carrying the ball in one hand for a few strides. My old teammate, Steve DeBerg, had a big season in 1990 with the Chiefs—23 touchdowns and only 4 interceptions in 444 attempts!—in part because he went back to using one hand on the play-action. DeBerg's running game allowed for this, though, because the Chiefs had deep handoff. Faster developing runs, like the ones we used in San Francisco, with backs hitting the holes quickly and linemen pulling, made anything one-handed a bit more risky.

A two-handed play fake involves a little sleight of hand. Say it's a run to the right, which means you'll be on the running back's left. Reach for his stomach while holding the ball with both hands. Transfer the ball to your right hand and leave your left hand in his stomach as if it's a regular handoff. Hide the ball from the line of scrimmage with your stomach. It's really not that hard, but most quarterbacks hate working on the running game during practice. They want to be a quarterback so they can throw—so when running drills are called, these guys say to the other quarterbacks, "Oh, no, you take it." At some point, probably during crunch time, they'll wish they did the reps.

It's not enough for the quarterback to be adept at faking the handoff. The running back has to fake, too. Much of the play-action, in fact, depends on the fake made by the back. If a quarterback does a great fake, and the back just lets his arms fall to his side, it's worthless. The back has to do the job of pretending as though he is covering the ball, exactly as he would if it were a real handoff. If he doesn't do that, it's a waste of time. Those little jab-type fakes don't fool anybody. The better the play-action fake, the better it helps both your running and passing games.

READING THE DEFENSE

You need to get to the point where, whatever the drop, you don't have to think about your feet. You'll need to be scanning the field and working through your receiver progression—which receiver is your first option, which is your

Montana keeps his eyes straight up field in this pre-season game against the Buffalo Bills. Looking straight downfield during your drop gives the defense no indication of where the pass is going.

second, and so on. In Pee Wee football, this progression may only be two options. In high school, it's usually three, and in college, four. In the pros, it could be as many as five. By the time you've taken your second step back from center you should already know who you'll be throwing to.

That's right, two steps. You should already know exactly where all your receivers should be. When you recognize the defense, you should know which of your guys will be open and which will be covered *before* the play really develops. If you wait too long to see who has *gotten* open— well, by that time he's not open anymore and you're on your back.

You do your best to read the defense at the line of scrimmage, before the ball is snapped—as we cover in Chapter 6. But when the play starts, many times, it's back to square one—those times when your preliminary read was incorrect, and you're staring at something completely unexpected.

Reading the defense during the drop is just one more reason why any quarterback who thinks he can do it alone will be in for a long day. You could be extremely adept at reading defenses, but that won't help you very much if your receivers are reading it differently. They'll be reacting to what they see, too, and adjusting their routes accordingly. If you haven't put in the time with them in practice, you won't always be on the same wavelength. They won't always be where you expect them to be, and when you're in the pocket, you don't have that second or two to find them.

Remember Steelers quarterback Neil O'Donnell in Super Bowl XXX against the Cowboys? He threw two interceptions that hit Cowboys' defensive back, Larry Brown, right between the numbers, without a Steeler receiver anywhere nearby. No one except Neil and his receiver knows exactly what happened, but this could very well have been a case of a quarterback and his receiver reading a defense differently.

In San Francisco, Dwight Clark was great at reading defenses. After a while, I could tell what he was going to do just by how he was running his route. That won't come immediately, but over time you will develop that kind of telepathy with your receivers if you all pay constant attention during games and are willing to put in the work during and after practice.

Reading defenses can't be taught completely. Yes, you need preparation, experience, and good vision. But some people just feel more comfortable with their instincts, while others hesitate. The *main thing* a quarterback needs to work on—or, in this case, stay away from—is looking to where you are going to throw the ball. Looking straight ahead is **very** important, especially from the top of your drop. If you don't look straight up the field on the first few steps—and instead you're looking where you want to go with the ball—you'll tip off the play. You should know where the ball is going, but if

Game Footage

You feel the ball slam against your right hand, laces right along your fingers. Your left hand clamps shut on it while you grip it with your right hand. You pivot on your left foot and step back with your right. Both hands are on the ball, you're holding it near your chest, elbows tucked in, and you're looking straight down-field.

It's a three-man rush, with eight dropping into coverage. Out of the corner of your eye you're watching the left cornerback. He's running with your primary receiver.

You crossover with the left, step with the right. You check the safeties. The free safety is cheating a few steps toward your split-end who is running a deep pattern toward the end zone. The strong safety is staying at home, deep right. The right corner is running with your split-end, too. That means double coverage.

You crossover with your left foot. Two inside linebackers are covering the short areas. You check your third receiver on the progression: your halfback on a comeback route. Will he break off his pattern and find the "seam" between the two linebackers?

You plant with the right. Your front hand pushes the ball back into throwing position. Your arm is cocked.

To be continued . . .

you stare down the receivers, everyone will notice. Some quarterbacks who don't feel comfortable with their abilities feel they have to make sure that they see what is happening, but all they're doing is telegraphing their throws.

Reading defenses is very difficult, but the more of it you do, the better you will get. Have you ever seen those chessmasters who play 40 games at once, moving from board to board? They only spend a few seconds on each game, yet they win all 40 games. It's not that their brain can process all that information that quickly. It's that they recognize "the board"—how their opponents' pieces are set up. And they know how to beat it. They've played so many games, they've seen it all before.

That happens in football, too, and it can be a great feeling—for the offense, anyway.

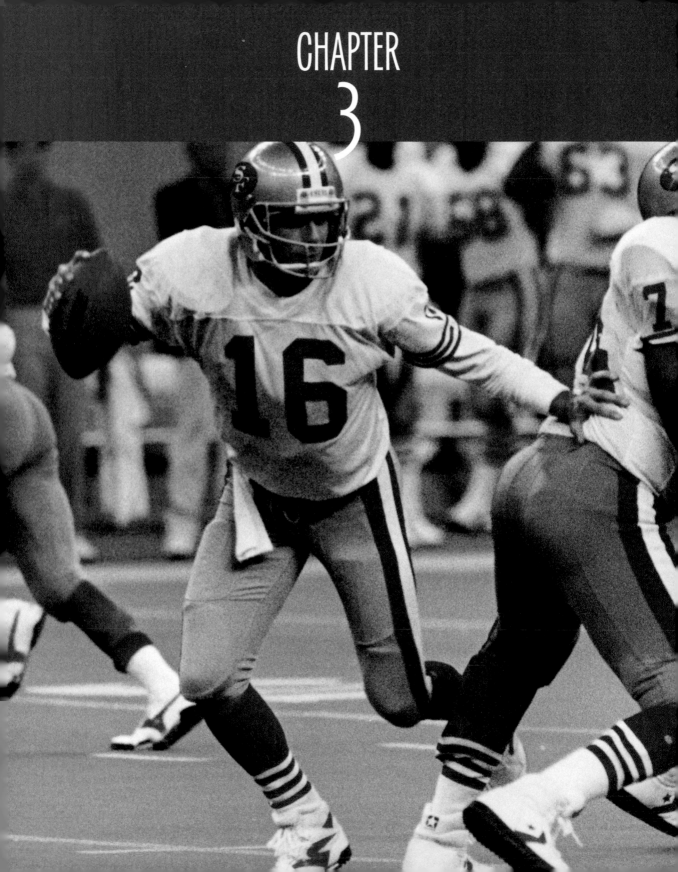

IN AND OUT OF THE POCKET

There is nothing more important for a young quarterback than to practice throwing the football. But you should know going in that when the plays get drawn up on the blackboard, the blocking scheme gives the quarterback plenty of time to stand in the pocket and choose which of the open receivers he wants to throw to, then deliver a fundamentally sound, picture-perfect strike. Well, when that play makes it from the blackboard to the playing field, your blocking could break down, your receivers could be covered, or you could be hounded out of the pocket by an unexpected blitz.

That's why we won't just cover the mechanics of throwing and the basic pass patterns. We'll talk about reading defenses, dealing with pass rushes, and handling smothering coverages, and, most importantly, throwing off-balance or on the run.

THROWING THE BALL

The fundamentals of throwing involve more than just your arm. A proper throw involves your feet, legs, hips, shoulders, elbows, hand, and fingers—all working together. You should protect your arm by stretching before you throw (see Chapter 8) and soft-tossing before you go all-out. Your warm-up should be at least 10–15 minutes.

The Grip

The first step to throwing a football is to get a proper-sized ball. Sometimes parents make the well-intentioned mistake of going out and finding for their kid the best football made, but for younger kids, an official-sized ball is just going to discourage them because it's too big. Kids should use footballs that are the right size for their hands. With all the drills we'll discuss later, you'll find you're better off with a few footballs than one really good one, anyway.

> "There's a difference between a quarterback coming away from the center and saying to himself, "I hope I can find my receiver," and a quarterback coming away saying, "You better stop this one. I'm putting it right there in his gut."
>
> —*Allie Sherman, former head coach of the New York Giants*

All quarterbacks hold the ball a little bit differently. Terry Bradshaw, for instance, used to hold the ball with his index finger all the way back, almost on the point. John Elway holds the ball fairly far back, too. As for me, I held it closer to the middle than that, my pinkie on the fifth lace and my ring finger on the second. My index finger was down toward the point and over the seam. My thumb was resting comfortably underneath, but not squeezing too hard—not too low, not too high. There's no right or wrong way to place your fingers. The closer to the middle you hold it, the more control you'll have. The farther back you go, the more power you can generate.

The ball should not be pressed tightly against your palm, but held on your fingertips. Even when you've worked well with the center, the ball will come to your hand in all sorts of directions. You have to find a way to get the proper grip quickly. The most important "hand and fingers" drill you can do is to practice picking up a ball the same way every time—with the grip that you use when throwing—until it becomes second nature.

When you throw, you don't want to hold the ball too tightly, or else you won't get that whip action out of your arm as you throw. It should be a constant, smooth grip, with a little tension, because you've got to be able to hang on to the ball. You can't squeeze it too much, because that's when you wind up getting too much flutter on the ball and losing control. That was my tendency—squeezing it too much, just from the tension of wanting to get it in there and make the completion.

Sometimes you are faced with bad weather, and you try to squeeze it even harder. Maybe that's why I may have been the worst rain-thrower who ever played the game. I just could not grip a wet ball, so any advice I have to offer should be taken with several grains of salt. Hopefully it will work better for you than it did for me.

With a slick ball, your instinct is to tighten your grip on it. You need to do the exact opposite. Loosen your grip a bit and be very deliberate in your throwing. Don't try to do things at top speed. It's just like driving—on a wet road, it's the sharp turns and the sudden stops that get you in trouble. Your mental approach is important, too. If you think throw-

(1) Montana gripped the ball close to the middle with his pinkie finger on the fifth lace and his ring finger on the second. This grip gave him excellent control of the ball, which was critical in running the 49er offense. (2) The space between Joe's palm and the ball indicates he's holding the ball in his fingers. Remember to eliminate tension in your grip. Holding the ball too tightly will decrease the velocity on your throw, turn a spiral into a lame duck and put increased strain on your arm.

ing in the rain is difficult, it will be. It might help to focus on the advantages a wet field gives your offense. Your receivers may have an easier time getting open. Your guys know where they're going and the defense doesn't, so who's more likely to slip?

Throwing in the wind isn't very fun either. The biggest thing you can do to help yourself—other than handing the ball off to Gale Sayers or Barry Sanders—is to throw spirals. The slightest wobble you get on your throws will be accentuated by the wind. A half-decent throw under normal conditions could turn out to be a big-time duck.

In short, trying too hard won't help you in dealing with the elements. If anything, it will take your mind off other things, namely the game plan. Another problem with trying too hard is that a tight grip will put more strain on your arm. If you feel any pain in your forearm and shoulder as you throw—or afterwards—chances are you're gripping the ball too tightly.

When you're done throwing, you should soak your shoulder and elbow in ice. Quarterbacks should ice after throwing all the time, no matter what their age. It helps keep

Joe begins his throwing motion by pointing his front shoulder at the target. He keeps his front shoulder closed as he draws the ball back to his ear. As he brings the ball back behind his head, Joe opens his hips and upper body to face his target. This allows him to put his entire body into the throw. As he brings his arm forward, the ball is pointing at the receiver. The ball is released just past his head, while his eyes remain locked on the target. The throwing hand turns over in the follow-through, with the thumb pointing down toward the ground.

A SOLID BASE

Want to know one place to start if you want to learn how to throw a football? Watch a tape of Nolan Ryan. Why should you be watching a pitcher? Nolan Ryan played longer than anyone in the history of Major League Baseball—as a fastball pitcher—and didn't blow out his arm until the age of 46 in what was supposed to have been the second-to-last start of his career. He could throw 100 miles per hour and was spared arm miseries—both for the same reason: he threw with his legs.

A quarterback needs to use his entire body to throw, too. Using your entire body to throw—driving with your legs, turning with your hips, and letting your arm trail your torso on the follow-through—will give you more zip and take the pressure off of your arm and elbow.

Joe leans back to throw one deep in the NFC championship game against the Dallas Cowboys in 1982. Notice his shoulders are not parallel to the ground. They are pointed slightly up, indicating he's about to fire a pass downfield.

inflammation down in the tendons and joints. Take care of your arm. If it hurts, it's trying to tell you something. Don't try to be a hero and play through it.

Everyone knows about pitchers blowing out their arms, but it happens to quarterbacks too. You ever hear of a guy named Greg Cook? Probably not. One of my coaches, Sam Wyche, played with him on the Bengals and Bill Walsh coached him. Cook led the AFL in passing *as a rookie* in 1969—in a league with Daryle Lamonica, Len Dawson, and Joe Namath! Well, Cook was trying to play through a shoulder injury, and it kept him out for the next three years. He only threw three more passes in his career.

The Throwing Motion

When it comes to throwing in a game, you'll be doing yourself a big favor if you've got the fundamentals down, what with everything else you have to be thinking about. Ask Terry Bradshaw, Joe Namath, Terry Hanratty, Troy Aikman, Dan Marino, Johnny Unitas. They'll all tell you that learning fundamentals early was the key.

I was more of a body-thrower than an arm-thrower. The trade-off is pretty simple: body-throwers can get more on the ball and save their arm some wear and tear; arm-throwers can release the ball more quickly. Unless you have an especially strong arm, you will probably need to be a body-thrower to get the ball downfield.

Here's how a body-thrower's motion should go.

1. Your front shoulder should be pointed toward your target, and your hips should be slightly closed.

2. As you step toward the receiver, you should be pushing back with your front hand to move the ball into throwing position by your ear—like a baseball catcher.

3. Point to your receiver with your non-throwing elbow.

4. Turn your hips, point your front foot toward the target, and let the ball follow behind.

5. Drive your front elbow down and through while pushing off with your back leg, the back foot pivoting toward your target.

6. The ball should be released just past your head, with your index finger the last thing off the ball.

7. You should land on your front heel with your knee bent slightly.

8. Your follow-through should leave all your weight on your front leg, rolling forward from your heel to your toe.

"Throwing over the top has everything to do with accuracy. And what controls the ball going over the top is your opposite shoulder. If your non-throwing shoulder comes open, the ball goes out. Watch a quarterback against the rush. If they come in and he opens his shoulder . . . as soon as he does this, throwing sidearm in a sense, away goes the accuracy."

— *Tom Martinez, College of San Mateo head coach*

9. Your throwing hand should end up at your opposite hip (right hand at the left hip), the thumb pointing down at the ground.

Throwing long is slightly different. Your shoulders won't remain parallel to the ground. As you step forward slightly with your plant foot, you should be dipping your back shoulder and raising your front shoulder. You need to push hard off your back leg when delivering the ball. Don't dip your back shoulder too much, or you'll be throwing straight up without much distance because the ball won't turn over.

Dan Marino is known for having one of the quickest releases in the history of the game. He is an arm-thrower, which allows him to shorten his front step and accelerate the turn of his hips and shoulders. If you can do it and still get some power on your throws, go for it—but it's harder on your arm and not many can do it well.

Here are some things to watch out for.

1. You don't want to let the ball get too far back when you plant your foot. It lengthens your delivery. This is yet another reason to carry the ball in two hands—it's easier to keep the ball by your ear as you set up to throw.

2. You don't want to turn the ball sideways as you draw it back. This is another reason to keep two hands on the ball. That way your front hand can guide the ball back so that the point is always going forward. The point should be aimed at your target throughout the delivery, so that when you throw, it comes off this way. If you've got it right, the ball should spin slightly off-center—nose up and to the right for a righty.

3. You want your shoulders and hips to work together. Opening your hips too soon will cause overthrows. Opening your shoulders too soon will diminish your accuracy.

4. You want your shoulders to be parallel to the ground (unless you're throwing long). Dropping your back shoulder will cause you to throw high, while dipping your front shoulder will cause low throws.

"Feet and legs are more important than [quarterbacks'] arms. Most people wouldn't think that. Kids need to develop their legs to have quick feet, and develop their hip area, because that's where all their strength is coming from, most of the time, when throwing a football."

—John Barnes, 1993 California coach of the year, Los Alomitos High School

5. You don't want to land on a stiff front knee. This keeps your weight from shifting through your delivery. It will cause you to throw short, while also putting enormous strain on your arm.

6. You don't want to land with the weight on the front of your foot or on your toes. This will cause you to throw the ball into the ground.

7. Be careful not to overstride; this lengthens your delivery, causes overthrows, and carries you into the pass rushers.

Most of the quarterback's mechanics will come with proper training, backed up with game experience. Provided you warm-up properly, your mechanics are good, and you stop if you start to feel pain, then I wouldn't worry about too much throwing. It's difficult for me to understand the way baseball teams use pitchers. Baseball coaches only let pitchers throw a certain amount between starts, rarely allowing the pitcher to throw as hard as possible. Quarterbacks—we throw as hard as we can a lot. If you watch our throwing motion closely, we are actually throwing screwballs. I question the handling of these baseball pitchers, especially after throwing so many passes during my career, in practice and during games. My elbow didn't give out until I was 35, and even then, I was able to came back from it and play until I was 38. I've talked with baseball pitchers about this, too, and most agree that the arm is pretty resilient if the proper mechanics are used.

These fundamentals are critical, but you'll learn quickly that you won't be able to step and follow through on every throw. In a game there is basically a wall in front of the passer. Sometimes you make the throw and your body can only go so far forward. You'll need to get used to that—not getting the complete follow-through all the time because of the rush. In other words, if you've got too long a stride, a pressure defense will help cure you of it.

There are plenty of drills you can do to improve your throwing. I threw a football at a tire hanging from a tree. If I hit the tire and it began swinging, then I had a moving target to throw at. Something else you can do by yourself is kicking

On Joe Montana's "tight wobble"—a not-exactly perfect spiral: "He had a little porpoise to (his throw), but the ball landed very softly in the receiver's hands. A lot of guys are throwing strikes, but people aren't catching them."

—Sam Wyche

Joe is shown practicing the on-the-knee drill. The drill isolates the middle and upper body, and teaches the importance of hip rotation.

The Physics of Football

"Gyroscopic stability." That's what the physicists call a spiral, and a tight one will spin about ten times per second. You can learn a lot about throwing a football from a physicist. For example, the tighter and quicker the spiral, the farther the football will fly. After all, the "drag" on a football can vary from .15 pounds to 1.5 pounds, depending on how it's thrown—nose-first in a tight spiral, or with the points to either side like a wounded duck.

In addition to a tight spiral, the release will have a great influence on the distance of the throw. To maximize distance, it should be released at a 10 degree angle from the ground. If the angle is increased, distance is sacrificed and hang-time is increased—which actually can be useful on some "touch" passes where you need to drop it over one line of coverage and in front of another.

Finally, the grip on the football will have an impact on how far it travels. Control—and spin—is increased when the ball is gripped near the middle. Force is increased when the ball is gripped near the back. That's one of the reasons John Elway can throw the ball so far—he can grip it near the back while still maintaining control over its path.

a soccer ball downfield and then trying to hit it with a pass. Passing drills can be boring, but if you practice with someone else, you can turn the drill into a competition. Establish targets to throw at, then keep track of how many tosses it takes to hit the target. Set up some garbage cans to throw at, and assign different point totals for each. See who can get the most points. Find other targets, too—use your imagination.

A more sophisticated drill is the *on-the-knee drill*. In this drill, you have your weight on your right knee with your left foot forward. You hold the football in front of your chest in both hands. You then throw at different targets—in front of you, and at angles to the left and right—which forces you to shift weight to your rear leg during your delivery. This is a good warm-up, and you don't need to throw hard to get something out of it. It will strengthen your arm and teach you how to use your body in the throw ("trunk rotation")—a lot more than a simple game of catch will do.

Do about 20 off one knee, then switch to the other. Then do it while on both knees—which is good practice for when you won't be able to step into the throw. Most of the time during a game, a quarterback is throwing off-balance in some way. The next time you watch an NFL game, count how many times a quarterback is able to deliver a ball with the perfect follow-through described here. Compare that to how many times he's forced out of his rhythm. Often there's no time, or there's a defender in your face, so making the perfect steps for a throw is out of the question. Similarly, there are times when following through is impossible. Learning to throw with only your body is vital.

Another drill is the *front-foot drill*. You throw while raising up on your toes. As a right-hander throws, he will shift his weight from his right foot to his left foot. This process forces you to throw overhand. If you have any tendency to come only three-quarters in your delivery, this will help cure you of it.

To be honest, I didn't really enjoy those drills, but I did them anyway. It was the game I enjoyed, and these helped me play better. Now, if you're not having fun during the games—well, maybe you shouldn't be out there.

Touch

Bill Walsh would preach patience to me when I was a young quarterback. Patience is probably never more important with any aspect of throwing than it is with "touch." Touch is the ability to put a ball *exactly* where you want—softly floating it over a defender, for example, rather than trying to throw the ball through defenders, as hard as you can, on every play.

With enough repetition, you can get to the point where you can make the ball do whatever you want on every throw. Eventually, you should be able to drop the ball right where you want it at least seven times out of ten—eight out of ten during practice. Touch is important for all quarterbacks, but especially for those who don't have a great arm.

The key to developing touch in practice is to pretend, right when you get the ball, that there is someone between you and your receiver. If you have someone to practice with, try tossing passes from the 10-yard line through the football

Developing touch is something that is acquired through repetition and drill work. Here, Joe practices dropping passes into a box. A quarterback can practice this drill by himself.

uprights to a receiver standing directly behind the center support. If you run out of people to practice with, you can always set up a box in your target area. Then try to drop the ball into the box. If you don't have a box, try aiming for a circle on the ground or a spot in the grass. You try to hit that spot, but you try to do it different ways. You can throw it hard sometimes, or you can throw it up over the top. That's why the box helps—you can actually drop the ball into the box on the throw, or at least practice doing so. If you throw it too hard, it will knock the box over. We figured this one out just playing around as kids. It probably started out with a trash can or something like that.

Jim Kelly, Troy Aikman, and Jeff Blake have all showed that you don't have to throw the ball hard every time to be successful. They all have excellent touch. Consider the touchdown pass we connected on at the end of Super Bowl

XXIII, when John Taylor caught the winning score in the closing seconds. I didn't throw that ball as hard as possible, but I did throw it as quickly as possible—in fact, it was probably the best pass I ever threw.

It's like a golf swing. The harder you swing doesn't necessarily equate to how far the ball will go, but your timing must be perfect.

Throwing on the Run

Few quarterbacks can consistently succeed through scrambling. Randall Cunningham did for a while, but teams eventually stopped blitzing him and made him beat them with his arm. That wasn't a style of play he was ever really comfortable

> "I've been playing this game for 18 years, and I haven't yet figured a way to get into the end zone when you're on your rear end."
>
> —Fran Tarkenton, one of the greatest scrambling quarterbacks in the history of the NFL

New York Giant Lawrence Taylor chases Randall Cunningham out of the pocket. Though Cunningham never enjoyed being hounded by linebackers, it was often beneficial to his game.

with—which is too bad, because at his best he was one of the game's most exciting players.

The threat of you taking off and running is certainly something you want the defense to be thinking about. After all, a good scrambler has to be treated as a sixth receiver by the defense. You don't have to be the fastest guy on the team to be able to buy yourself some time in the pocket. There have been a lot of great improvisers who wouldn't win too many foot races.

For all this talk about my footwork and elusiveness, I really didn't rack up all that many yards rushing—an average of about ten per game. That's no big deal. There are plenty of guys who've picked up more rushing yardage in less time than me—Roger Staubach, Terry Bradshaw, Fran Tarkenton, Steve Young, John Elway, Bobby Douglass, Greg Landry, Randall Cunningham, Steve Grogan, Warren Moon, Joe Theismann, Ken Anderson, Archie Manning—and that's by no means a complete list. The point is, I scrambled to complete a pass—to get the ball to someone who knew what to do with it.

Throwing on the run is something that I don't think can be practiced too much. You can do what's called the *throw-on-the-run drill*. You have two quarterbacks ten yards apart, running along parallel lines, and throwing the ball to each other. This will reinforce two important things about throwing on the run: squaring your shoulders to the receiver before you throw, and *not* leading the receiver when you're both running in the same direction. When you're both moving the same way, throw it *at* him. If you're having trouble hitting your receivers when you're on the dead run, it may not be because of anything you're doing wrong with your shoulders, hips, or arm. You may be running on your heels instead of your toes, which is much more jarring on your eyes and makes it more difficult to focus on your target.

Another good drill is the *escape drill*. In this one, you will drop back to pass and be directed by a coach to move left, right, or up to simulate eluding a rush. At some point, the coach will raise his hand, and you will have to immediately throw the ball. This teaches you to always be in position to throw, despite what may be going on all around you. Sam Wyche used to run this drill—and he'd throw tackling dummies at us as we threw—to get us used to being harassed by pass rushers.

"I wasn't bad as a scrambler or ball-handler, but after watching Montana play I don't think I could carry the guy's helmet. I've seen some great quarterbacks—Otto Graham, Bob Waterfield, Norm Van Brocklin—and I'd say Montana ranks with the top two or three to ever play the game. When things break down and people start to scatter, he's at his best. He can get out of trouble and do things no other quarterback can do. He makes plays out of nothing. That's a gift."

—Frankie Albert, former 49ers quarterback

Montana made a career out of throwing on the run. He often threw off
the wrong foot, but did so deliberately with pinpoint accuracy.

The Catch. Here is the play that made Joe Montana a household name and launched the 49ers into their Super Bowl era. Wide receiver Dwight Clark's job was to slide along the back of the end zone as Joe rolled out to the right. Montana found him and the rest, as they say, is history.

> "It was a play we always ran. My job was to find Joe and, once he found me, slide along the end line. By the time he saw me, he was desperate. . . . There's no other place Joe could have thrown the ball. If it had been anywhere else, Everson Walls would have made a play on it."
>
> —Dwight Clark

I first learned these fundamentals from my dad, Joe, Sr. He made it seem like a game. He adapted the throw-on-the-run drill by having the quarterbacks throwing to each other as we ran half-circles and circles. Then he had us running these circles in the opposite direction so that we'd get comfortable changing directions. When you saw me throwing on the run or off the wrong foot—like The Catch—that was Joe, Sr.

It was a sprint-out to the right, but the primary receiver (Freddie Solomon) was covered, and the Dallas pass rush was closing in. I had to put it up there where, if Dwight couldn't get it, no one could. I was moving backward, off-balance, and throwing on the toes of my right foot with my left foot off the ground. Not exactly perfect form, but that's where all those drills paid off. I never saw Dwight catch it until later on instant replay. It was an amazing grab—especially for someone who was sick as a dog at the time.

PASS PATTERNS

A quarterback must first learn the basic pass routes—especially *slants*, *quick outs*, *hooks*, and *crossing patterns* across the middle, which are the plays the majority of offenses will use on a regular basis. You must become proficient at throwing the ball accurately without fear of an interception. A lot of this depends on timing.

There really are only a few patterns. After all, there are only so many ways a receiver can run downfield. Besides, it's not the pattern that gets a guy open. What matters is who's running them, and when.

Short Patterns

There are four primary short patterns, with three of them thrown off a 3-step drop: the *quick out*, *hitch*, and *slant*. The *square out* is thrown off a 5-step drop. Timing is vital on all of them.

In a *quick out*, the receiver goes downfield five yards then breaks toward the sideline. The quarterback will be delivering the ball as the receiver makes his break. In a *hitch*, the receiver goes down five yards, then breaks inside and back toward the line of scrimmage. Here, again, the ball will be delivered as the receiver makes his break. But you have to be particularly aware of the perils receivers face when they go underneath. Say it's first-and-ten. You think you can hit the receiver for eight yards over the middle, but it's tight, and throwing his way could get him crushed. Dump it to the back on a swing pass instead. Take the second-and-six and keep your receiver in the game.

In a *slant*, the receiver goes down about five yards, then breaks diagonally across and down the middle of the field. This is one of the most difficult passes to throw, especially on a cold day. Most quarterbacks don't like warming up with a slant because it takes such good arm strength. You don't have the luxury of getting your body underneath the pass, because you don't have time to take that extra hitch step before you plant and throw. This made the slant harder for me than throwing downfield. You just have to pick a hole and trust that the receiver will turn in time to see the ball. Usually, you have to throw it before the receiver is ready, so you're not really throwing to the receiver—you're throwing to a hole behind a defender.

A slant in man-to-man coverage is a lot easier to deliver. It used to be that some teams wouldn't even try to throw a slant into zone coverage—but maybe the sight of Jerry Rice or

"A young quarterback should learn how to throw the simpler routes. Those are your bread and butter. You won't get many picked off if you make sure your receivers are moving back toward the ball and you know your underneath coverage."

—Daryle Lamonica

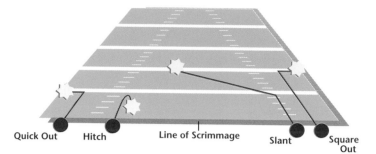

Quick Out   Hitch   Line of Scrimmage   Slant   Square Out

Timing is integral in executing short patterns. The quarterback has to know precisely where the receiver will be at any given time, and also needs to be aware of the speed and quickness of each individual receiver. The time it takes Jerry Rice to run a five-yard hitch may take less time than another receiver.

"There are some guys who can see an opening in the defense but can't do anything about getting the ball in there. There are some guys who can throw the ball, but they never get that opening. And then there are the handful of guys who can see the opening—see the coverage and the pattern within the coverage—*and* get it in there quickly and accurately. It's not easy, even if Joe made it look that way most of the time. That's why his guys always ran so well after the catch. He wouldn't just get the ball in there, he'd do it with such accuracy—darn near perfect strikes. They wouldn't even have to break stride to catch the ball."

—*John Madden*

John Taylor breaking into the open changed that. On a slant, the receiver is passing through what we call zone holes. You try to get him during the first hole. If you must go to the second hole, you've probably been looking that way too long, and people will converge on the location. You'll need to let it go when you see the first hole open up. You want to hit the receiver early, because he will be going into an area where a lot of people are coming at him quickly.

Rice and Taylor should have their pictures next to the word "slant" in any football textbook. They excelled because of their ability to run with the ball after the catch. Their size helped, too, because a lot of the defensive backs were shorter and would play looser than they did on other coverages to make sure they could contain the play. If the defender missed a hit after a reception, though, Jerry and John would bounce right off. These two would turn short passes into big gains because of their ability to run, take a hit, and not go down.

They were the big difference between the '81 Super Bowl team that beat the Bengals and the '88 and '89 Super Bowl teams that beat the Bengals and Broncos. Those later teams had offenses that really put a lot more pressure on the opposing defenses. Jerry Rice and John Taylor were two of the main reasons for that.

On a *square out*, the receiver goes down about ten yards, then cuts toward the sidelines. The ball is thrown before the receiver makes his break, but unlike the quick out, you are throwing the ball a lot farther without really being able to get

John Taylor celebrates a game-winning touchdown late in the 4th quarter. Taylor took a short slant pass from Montana and turned it into a 46-yard scoring play.

your body completely into the throw (as you would off a 7-step drop or a 5-step drop with a hitch). If you don't have a real strong arm, then you better be quick and have great timing. Even if you do have a great arm, you still better have your timing down, or it will be the cornerback's chest you'll be bruising with your fastball.

This pattern also illustrates how important teamwork is to passing. Two quarterbacks could throw the identical square out, and one could be caught for a 12-yard gain while the other could be picked off and returned for a touchdown. The difference: how the receiver runs his pattern. If he doesn't cut hard on his break and just kind of rounds it off, it will be easier for the corner to stay right with him. If the corner is there, you can't complete that pass. Since you're throwing on the break, you have to trust that your receiver will make a sharp cut that will give him two steps on his defender.

The square out is about as tough to execute as the slant, but, also like the slant, this pattern is really hard to stop if the ball is thrown correctly and on time—because there is nothing the defender can do about it unless he's playing loose. If he is playing honestly, the cornerback or the safety or even the outside linebacker will have a very difficult time defending the square out because a sharp cut will put him on his heels.

Longer Patterns

The longer patterns can be a bit more complicated—and there are a lot more of them—simply because the receiver has more time and room to maneuver. They're run off of four basic routes: the *crossing pattern, deep square out, post,* and *streak.*

On a *crossing pattern,* the receiver goes down 15 to 20 yards, then breaks straight across the middle of the field. It's thrown off a 7-step drop, and in zone coverage, it may require a touch pass to get it over a linebacker and in front of a safety.

A variation on this play is the *deep cross,* which involves an earlier break and an angled cross, going from one side of the field to the other—rather than going up 15 yards and straight across the middle. After about five yards, the receiver starts angling across the field and ends up about 15 yards deep. And there is the *shallow cross,* which is thrown off a 5-step drop. On this route, the receiver starts about one yard deep and ends up six or seven yards deep on the other side of the field.

These are a bit tougher to throw than the standard cross, because not only are you throwing to a guy crossing the field, but he's gaining yardage on you. That is one of the things a quarterback hates having to deal with. When you are trying to throw the ball into seams and the guy is moving down-field, that's tough. You'd rather see him coming back to the ball so that if two defenders are closing in on it, he has a good chance to come between those guys and make the reception.

The square out is tough enough to throw, but the *deep square out* is even harder. It's run just like a square out, only 15 to 20 yards downfield. You need to throw before the break and hit the receiver at the sideline. If you have an especially

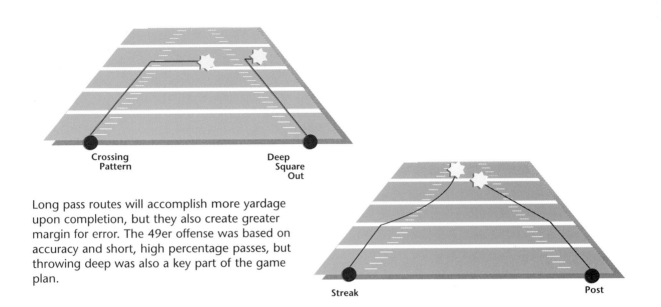

Crossing Pattern

Deep Square Out

Streak

Post

Long pass routes will accomplish more yardage upon completion, but they also create greater margin for error. The 49er offense was based on accuracy and short, high percentage passes, but throwing deep was also a key part of the game plan.

strong arm, you can hold the ball a bit longer before you throw it. If you don't, you have to trust that the receiver will make a sharp cut and get open. Here is where an acrobatic receiver can really help a quarterback. If you can count on him to plant both feet (or one foot in lower levels) and lean over the sideline to make a catch, then you can consistently throw the ball even more to the outside and cut down on the likelihood that this pass might get picked off and returned all the way.

On a *post* pattern, the receiver runs straight down the field for about ten yards, then cuts toward the goalpost. If you throw this off a 5-step drop, you've got a better chance of keeping a safety from moving into coverage. You may also throw this off a 3-step drop if you are facing an all-out blitz. I started throwing this a lot more when we added Jerry Rice to our offense, and he's still making a living on that pattern today. How many times are defenses going to let Jerry go to the post before someone says, "Hey, you know he does that an awful lot. Don't you think we can stop him?"

The *deep post* is not really a timed throw. It's a good option when there is no free safety in the area—or if you see man-to-man coverage and the receiver has beaten his defender downfield. There is also a *timed-post*, which is almost like throwing a slant, except you're working off a 5-step drop. You're still hitting the hole in the zone, but this time it's more like 15 yards downfield, at least. It's a nice route, because it keeps the defense off balance. They don't expect a ball thrown that deep on the inside. Once I got to that fifth step in my drop, I would wish I had a little more arm strength, because I couldn't always get my body into those throws.

There is also something called a *post corner* or *shake*. The receiver runs a post, but about five yards after cutting toward the goal post, he will cut back again toward the corner of the end zone.

Your speedy receivers love to run the *streak* or *go* pattern. It's basically "going long," like you do in the back yard, with a break to the outside after about ten yards. An inability to cover this pattern against a speedy receiver may force a lot of teams to play zone. I threw this pass off a 5-step drop with a hitch, because if I tried this off a 7-step drop I would under-throw the receiver. Some quarterbacks can throw this off a 7-step drop because they've got cannons for arms, and it gives them an extra second to make certain that their man is open.

The deep ball down the sidelines is the toughest pass to complete. And since Bill Walsh *hated* incompletions, we didn't throw too many. Still, you have to throw deep some-times, even if it's just to keep the defense honest. That's what we did the first time we played the Giants in the playoffs, back in 1981. We knew we had to stretch their defense, or their linebackers would have clamped down on us—like they did when they beat us in 1985 and 1986. Linebackers are looking for any excuse to play closer to the line of scrimmage, so you have to get their attention if you want them deeper in the secondary. The occasional bomb will do that.

The *comeback* is simply a streak pattern that is broken off toward the sidelines after about 20 yards. A *hook* is like a *comeback*, only the receiver is curling into the middle of the field—often into a seam in the zone. Sometimes your receiver will choose to break off a streak, and run a hook or comeback, based on his read of the defense. Many times when you see a quarterback throw a pass that lands with no receivers in the area and you scream, "To who?" at your television set, it's because the receiver broke off his route, while the quarterback did not read the defense the same way.

Roger Craig was difficult to contain coming out of the San Francisco back-field as a receiver. He often turned short swing passes into first downs.

Outlet Pass

An outlet pass could also be called a last resort. It's a short, "dump-off" pass that you know you can go to if everyone else is covered. Your primary outlet pass is a *swing*. You'll be throwing this one off-balance a lot, because it's usually thrown when everyone else is covered and the pocket is collapsing. Off-balance or not, you still have to deliver the ball on target. If the running back has to stop, or go back-ward, he has no advantage at the point of reception. You want the back to catch the ball on the run so it feels like second nature—he becomes a running back with the ball in the open field. You need the right type of back to pull this off. You can't have somebody who the first tackler is going to bring down. You need someone with the elusiveness of a

Roger Craig, a big running back with good moves who can accelerate fast. That's how we were able to win three of our Super Bowls.

In the West Coast Offense, the running back doesn't need to be a great runner, but he has to be a good runner, and an even better pass receiver. That's a big responsibility. A quarterback will go back to pass and look for his first and second receivers. Usually, the running backs are part of his second or third read. That type of outlet option can make the difference in a championship season.

Screen Pass

Like the play-action fake and the draw play, the *screen* pass is another play that requires good acting to deceive the defense. It's a dump-off, but not like a swing. On a screen, you sit back and intentionally draw the defense in. Your receiver is sitting back and pretending to be in on protection, while your linemen let their rusher through after acting like they're trying to block them. If you pretend to look terrified by the sight of an unimpeded rush, good. Drop back a few steps and look frantically for a receiver. That will only help "sell" the play. If you don't, you're hanging out there without blockers or an outlet. Your "blocking back" will be setting up behind the linemen, ready to catch the ball and be escorted down-field. You may have to throw a jump pass to get the ball over the pass rush—or even toss it sidearm to get it through—but it doesn't have to look pretty. It just has to get there.

Taking Care of Your Receivers

If you think passing accurately is hard, it *will* be hard. If you can visualize it with confidence, then it becomes second nature, and you'll demand perfection of yourself—instead of the coach demanding it first.

Ideally, you want to hit the receiver in stride. Sometimes you might intentionally throw a ball to a receiver, rather than in front of him, if you want to keep from bringing him into another zone area. This way he can stop and sit down in the seam of a zone.

Whether the ball was caught on the run or not, we were never satisfied with our throwing if the receiver had to out-stretch his arms to make the catch. We didn't want the guys to have to make a "thumbs-in" catch. Most receivers want it

The quarterback should always be conscious of where his receivers can best handle catching the football. Fortunately for Montana, he could throw the ball just about anywhere and Jerry Rice would come down with it.

in the stomach so they can protect their ribs—and you catch those balls "thumbs out." In addition to keeping your receivers in one piece, this usually means that they can protect the ball by keeping their body between the defender and the pass.

Another way you can help out your receiver is to not look at him. You'll have to look his way eventually, but the longer you can hold off from making that look, the better chance you have of getting the ball there without a big collision. The longer you look at him, the more pressure you are putting on your receiver—not just to catch the football, but also to take the big hit. Not only could it knock the ball loose, but it could get him hurt.

Of course, there will be times when you are pressured and unable to throw perfectly. In this case, the receiver must earn the catch—along with his paycheck or scholarship or letterman's jacket. Our guys never had to dive too much, because if we threw the ball too far in front of them, we'd get yelled at by Bill Walsh. Bill wanted the ball 6 to 12 inches in front of the jersey numbers, with no exceptions. On short patterns he even wanted us to be able to hit a guy on the left or right number, so we could tell them which way to turn to elude a defender.

Each pass requires a different throw, but most receivers will tell you that the easiest to catch is a soft toss with a tight spiral. It's hard to catch a ball that's drilled, but what your receivers really want from you is to simply throw the ball their way. Sometimes that's trickier than it sounds, especially if you're in an offense where the ball gets spread around like it was in San Francisco. Warren Moon had the same situation in Houston when he ran the run-and-shoot with four wide receivers. He told them he'd get the ball to all of them by the end of the first quarter, figuring that would keep their heads in the game. Other times, it's just a matter of being creative and using what you've got. Back in the late '50s and early '60s, the 49ers had a 6'3" receiver named R.C. Owens, who was a great leaper. Eventually, he and quarterback Y.A. Tittle figured out that all Tittle needed to do was throw the ball up for grabs in the end zone and let Owens go get it. That was the birth of the "alley-oop."

Practice and playing together is the key for a quarterback and his receivers. After a while, you will be able to just feel things. You can tell by the way a receiver runs, for instance, where he is going to break or how sharp he is going to be coming out of it. That's an edge for you. The last thing you should be doing is taking too long to think about what is happening. Obviously, there is a certain amount of information-processing taking place—but with enough patience, it should become second nature.

There is no one right way to throw a pass. You have to treat every throw differently, visualizing each one. You have to see the play develop before each throw. You can't simply go out there and throw it the same way ten times in a row. You have to say things to yourself like, "O.K., this is what's happening now. I've got to throw it over this guy's head and drop it in there, between this guy and that guy." If you train the mind to act in this manner, it will help the physical skills, too.

THE POCKET

You should already know where your receivers are going to be on any given play. That means that, as you drop back into the pocket, you'll be spending most of your time reading the defense, trying to elude a pass rush, and looking for a way to beat the coverage.

Reading the Defense

When it comes to reading defenses, people confuse seeing the field with *knowing* the field. You have to *know* where everybody is. Then, when you see something develop, it enables you to come back to some place quickly. All the time you know what is going to happen and what is taking place. Vision helps, but that will do little good without the knowledge of the field.

Sound hard? Well, a quarterback needs to make good reads 95–98% of the time to be successful. During an average NFL season, the combined total of accurate reads made by quarterbacks across the league is probably about 85–90%. To make good reads, it helps to have great players around you. Take Troy Aikman; not only is he a very smart quarterback with good fundamental skills and leadership ability, but he also has great receivers on each side and a great big line. So he's got the time to make great reads.

The key to making good reads is to get used to seeing defenses. There's really no way to practice, aside from doing it. Even if you see a "three-deep zone"—which we discuss in detail in Chapter 6—that's still only going to tell you to go to one area, and that area might be one entire side of the field. Then you have to make another decision, such as which guy to throw to in that area. Throw a new offensive system on top of that, and it can be very difficult for a quarterback—especially a young one.

The coach's game plan will, or should, prepare you for deciding what to do with the ball. If the information is processed accurately, the defense will pretty much tell you where the ball can be thrown as you drop back. That's what usually dictates your decisions. In that sense, it's not so much which receiver gets open, as it is which receiver is the defense unable to cover. At least that's how I looked at it.

"Let's just say it would help a quarterback's career if he could make intelligent decisions."

—Jack Tatum, former Raiders defensive back

"Joe always knows where everybody is, or should be, on a given play. He has fantastic downfield vision and instinct. That is the difference between being a mechanical man and a potentially great quarterback. So far, he has done some things we didn't expect to happen until next year or maybe even 1983. But we're not complaining about it."

—Bill Walsh, 1981

Even with pressure coming from both sides, Montana maintains his focus, and looks for an open receiver downfield.

"People don't see the mistakes of a defensive lineman. . . . Learning the quarterback trade is a difficult thing because you're out there in full view, and if you throw an interception, everyone sees it. They might not know why it happened, or if it even was the quarterback's fault. But they'll blame him and they'll remember."

—Chuck Noll

Sometimes you call a play that literally plays into the defense's hands, but you fail to check off at the line and call an audible. If you know it's a bad play, the best thing to do is take what you can and not try to do the impossible. This is where a lot of quarterbacks get into trouble. They stick with a bad play and try to make it work, as opposed to letting the ball fall. Incompletions are a lot better than interceptions. In other words, don't get hung up on your completion percentage. "W's" are the only stats that matter, anyway, even if they aren't included in the quarterback ratings.

Those ratings don't tell the whole story, anyway. For one thing, not all incompletions are created equal. An incompletion could be a drop by one of your receivers, a pass poorly thrown by you, or a heave out of bounds to stop the clock or avoid a sack. The rating looks at all of them the same way, though. The same is true with interceptions. Some are picked on the last play of a half on a "hail mary," others are tipped by receivers on passes that should have been caught; some end up in a defender's arms because the receiver fell down or ran the wrong route, and others are bad passes by the quarterback. Another misleading quarterback statistic is rushing yardage. How much of that yardage was gained because a quarterback gave up on the play too early and took off running?

If you want to know who the good quarterbacks are, watch the passes they complete on off-balance throws under a heavy rush. Watch the first downs they get on third-and-long, passing into heavy coverage. Listen to what their teammates have to say about them. And check the final score.

PASS RUSH

The pass rushers have the same objective as the rest of the defensive unit: to make you feel uncomfortable, to make you do what you don't want to do. They go about this by trying to sack you, knock you down after a pass, or at least make you run for your life. Standing in the pocket in the face of a heavy rush has been compared to auto racing, and that's not too far off. Personally, I always thought it was more like standing in the middle of a freeway.

It's been about 20 years since Steelers linebacker Jack Lambert suggested that quarterbacks should wear skirts. Nowadays, quarterbacks are built like him (6'4", 220 pounds), and linebackers are built like the guys who used to play defensive end, only faster. Since Lambert's time, Lawrence Taylor reinvented the outside linebacker position and pretty much guaranteed that every defense you face will have a hard-charging linebacker coming at you from your blindside. Finally, Buddy Ryan established an all-out pressure defense that loaded up the bodies at the line, daring the offensive line to block them all and forcing the quarterback to do things more quickly than he'd like. Linebackers are welcome to stand in against this stuff any Sunday, but I think they'd want that skirt to be armor-plated.

No point in sugar-coating it—it hurts to get stuck by a pass rusher. For a quarterback though, it's not the hitting that causes most injuries. It's the part afterward. That's when

On rushing the passer: "It's an art. It's also a car accident."

—Bruce Smith, defensive end

On eluding the pass rush: "It's amazing what the human body can do when chased by a bigger human body."

—Jack Thompson, former quarterback

Montana stands in and gets ready to deliver a pass when he knows he's about to get hit. It's not easy to do, but it's part of the job description.

people get hurt. Go back and look at the videotapes of injuries suffered by quarterbacks. It's when they hit the ground that most of them get hurt. The worst is when you get sandwiched into the ground, taking all that weight on your shoulders and chest.

Unfortunately, there is no avoiding getting hit, and there is no way to teach you how to take it—you just have to learn the proper way to fall, which most quarterbacks figure out on their own. The most important way to prepare for it is mentally, not physically. The driver who walks away from a car accident is often the one who didn't see it coming and who didn't tense up. A quarterback has to be the same way. It's not easy, but you have to relax and go with the flow.

There are other things you need to do, despite what that logical side of your brain is telling you to do: step up, remain calm, don't give up on the play. In the face of outside pressure, you need to move *forward*, stepping up into the pocket. It's an unnatural reaction, but you have to do it. The outside rushers' momentum will carry them right past you if you step up. Second, you have to keep your poise. The defense wants to see what they call "happy feet"—the quarterback who nervously shuffles his feet when the pressure heats up. That's not going to help you deliver the ball quickly. Maintain your footwork and throwing position, shoulders perpendicular to the line of scrimmage. Remember your receiver progression—especially what we call the "hot" receiver, the one ready for a quick pass. Complete a few of these and you'll grow more and more confident about standing in against a rush. Finally, don't just take off and run every time you get rushed. It's tempting, but you can't get in the habit of giving up on the plays. You might even have a lot of success running the ball, but eventually, opposing defenses will get wise to this. They might assign a linebacker to shadow you, as they try to take away your running and force you to beat them with your throwing. If you've been running all the time, you won't be prepared to direct a passing attack.

There are a number of ways a pass rush can try to disrupt your game. Here's how I tried to deal with each.

The Inside Push

An inside push totally disrupts a passer who doesn't move around a lot. The hardest thing for a quarterback to get away from is a defensive linemen who gets freed up the middle immediately after the snap. You can get away from most anything but a push up the middle. This is how Jim Burt took me out back in the '86 playoffs. The only way to get away from it is to get outside the pocket as quickly as you can.

Blindside Cornerback Blitz

The toughest blitz for a quarterback is always the cornerback coming from the blindside, because it is so difficult to see, let alone detect. Ask anyone who has played Pittsburgh in the past few seasons. These blitzes are often disguised well. Defenses roll their cornerbacks a lot to play bump-and-run; if you make your living with a receiver on the left-hand side, the defense will roll the cornerback up in there, pretending to

"The quarterback who shows the most poise in getting the ball off quickly is the most difficult for me to handle. Troy Aikman does a good job of getting rid of the ball, so you don't have time to get to him. Aikman, Dan Marino, and Joe—they get rid of the ball quickly. They don't just stand back there, but they also have poise when doing all of this."

—Reggie White, All-Pro defensive end

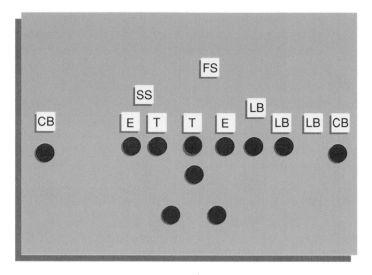

As you can see from the diagram, the most difficult aspect of facing the 46 Defense was that the quarterback never knew who would be blitzing. Ryan's pressure defense could take offensive units right out of their game plan.

bump the receiver, then come at you. It's impossible to see, so all you can do is know a team's tendencies and watch a lot of film to find the best way to burn them when they do it. Connecting for big gains against this blitz is the only way to get them to stop doing it.

All-Out Pressure

The toughest defensive packages we faced dealt with all-out pressure. Rather than rushing four linemen and dropping three linebackers into coverage, these defenses might send all seven guys after the quarterback. They might even blitz a safety, too. For the quarterback, you want to take advantage of anything and everything you see, but that is nearly impossible when faced with all-out pressure. Even if your offense is geared to completing a high percentage of passes like ours was, this kind of pressure will disrupt that.

We used to hate facing Philadelphia, Chicago, Houston, and Arizona when Buddy Ryan was implementing his pressurized 46 Defense with those teams. On the one hand, we felt there was a better opportunity for us to make big plays in these matchups. On the other hand, we knew the percentages of completions would be a lot lower than normal. The key, then, was to be patient, sit back, and wait for openings to be created. This was rough, especially when we were at the point with the 49ers and the Chiefs when getting completions was just about a given. Then came Buddy and his crazy fronts that drove the offensive coaches batty.

The full-on pressure allowed less time to throw, obviously, so you knew there was less time for the receiver to get open and rarely any time to complete a proper release. There were some other difficulties it posed: all three linebackers would be lined up opposite our tight end, so you never knew who was blitzing and who was on coverage; the guards couldn't come over to help out on these linebackers, because they were occupied by a defensive lineman; and the strong safety might be coming on a blitz up the middle, between the two defensive tackles. Now Buddy tells me he would even have his left end rush slow so that I couldn't step or move outside, away from the linebackers. This resulted in a lot of knock-downs—of both my passes *and* me.

I could handle just about every type of front, but the 46 was always the toughest. To combat this defense, we wouldn't simply shorten the quarterback's drops. We would shorten the receivers' routes, too. You then take just a couple of steps after the snap, and the receiver cuts sooner. The running backs were told to stay in at this point, too, which helps with protection—but limits the quarterback's options.

You'll get hit more in this situation, too, but that isn't the toughest part of it. You want to be precise, yet you need to understand that the defense is going to win a portion of the battles. That's why you see a lot more pressure now than in the past. The rules have changed to help the receiver, so defenses are willing to come hard and run the risk of getting burned rather than slowly bleeding to death.

Regardless of whether the defense is pushing up inside, sending defensive backs on your blindside, bringing all-out pressure, or simply taking on your linemen one-on-one, there will be times when the guys up front are having a tough day. The better you know your receivers and the quicker you can get the ball off, the more chances you'll have to stave off the defense. You'll save yourself some punishment, for one—and two, you'll help out your receiver by getting him the ball

As the pocket begins to close, Montana dumps off a pass to his fullback. Montana was a very patient quarterback. He would take the short gain rather than force a ball into coverage downfield.

sooner. He won't always have to catch it in traffic. With guys like Rice and Taylor, you never knew what could happen on even the shortest of passes.

Coverage

It doesn't necessarily take 15 pass plays for a quarterback to get into a rhythm. You can actually do it in one offensive series. You start to see how the pass rush, protection, and coverage is going to be, and you know exactly what needs to be done. It also doesn't take that long for a defense to put you on your heels, no matter what you try. The biggest thing for a quarterback, then, is to avoid forcing things and making the defense's job easier.

When people think about defense, they tend to focus on the pressure it brings. A fierce pass rush will force you out of the pocket, but so will excellent pass coverage. Your offensive linemen won't be able to keep a pass rush away from you forever if you don't have anyone to throw to.

As you move to higher levels of play, the defenders just get bigger, quicker, and more talented. There are some cornerbacks in the NFL now who can play a receiver man-to-man for the first few strides, then drop back into a zone. That's not easy. Quicker defenders mean smaller holes in zones. When facing that kind of challenge, you need to be prepared. You need to know the defense's strengths and weaknesses coming into the game, and you need to pick up on important details as the game progresses: who's tired, who's fresh, who's better at zone coverage, who's an excellent man defender, and who's playing tentatively because of a pass interference call.

Patience is also vital when you're faced with multi-defensive back formations. This is another relatively recent trend, with coaches throwing five, six, seven, and even eight defensive backs into some coverages. Some teams play what is called a nickel formation (five defensive backs) so much nowadays that it's become their base formation. This makes it much more difficult for you to find those holes in the defense to throw to—especially when you consider the new breed of defensive back: big, fast, and versatile. They have a lot more range than in the past. Their recovery speed enables them to react much more quickly to what the receivers are doing on a particular play. This is where a quarterback's patience comes in so handy. You must be willing, in this case, to take things underneath, otherwise this type of coverage will force you to make a bad throw.

This is where a lot of quarterbacks get into trouble. They don't want to take the short one and they try to force it into coverage for more yardage. Don't get greedy. If your primary receiver is open in the flat, take it. Don't hold out for a secondary receiver to get open further downfield.

"Coach, he was the only man open."

—*Johnny Lujack, Notre Dame quarterback and 1947 Heismann Trophy winner, explaining why he had thrown three interceptions to the same defensive back*

THE RED ZONE

You could look it up. During Joe's time, San Francisco was 14-5 in postseason, outscoring their opponents 498-326. But their opposition out-kicked them by a wide margin, 32 field goals to 20. That's not a knock on their kickers, but a tribute to the offense and defense.

With Joe, the 49ers led the NFL in points twice (1987 and 1989), but never in field goals. They kicked a lot of them in 1988, but that was an unusual season. They won it all that year, but at one point were 6-5, banged up, and basically running in place. They peaked at the right time—in the playoffs—once their offense stopped stalling out in the red zone.

Montana throws a short, sideline pass during the 49ers' Super Bowl XIX victory over the Dolphins. Montana was named MVP after throwing three touchdown passes—all to running backs.

The Red Zone

Everything changes once the quarterback is inside the opposition's 20-yard line (the "red zone"). Many teams are able to move the ball between the 20s without much difficulty, but they can't punch it in. Those are the teams that kick a lot of field goals and lose some games they should win.

There are some very good reasons why teams run into trouble in close. For one thing, the defense starts doing things differently. For some defenses, it almost becomes a pride thing. Like the Giants, who had that bend-but-don't-break approach, and who seemed to become personally offended by the idea that you might want to get to their end zone.

A lot of times, you go straight down the field against one type of defense and then you have to adapt to something totally different. You start to see a lot more blitzes. With no threat of a long-gainer, defenses are more willing to take risks. The quarterback should not only expect that, but also anticipate the man coverage which usually goes with the blitz. If you can keep your poise against a heavier rush, you should be able to find someone open. Unfortunately, some quarterbacks get rattled and throw those back-breaking end zone interceptions.

Other teams have success playing zone inside the 20-yard-line. The defense will drop everybody into coverage and rush only a few. They'll give you more time to throw and put their manpower into reducing your throwing lanes. Then it's up to you to find a hole. When you do, it won't be very big.

Game Footage

You are ready to follow through with a strike to your halfback on a comeback route when you see him slip and fall. You pull the ball in, both hands back on it, shoulders still perpendicular to the line of scrimmage, your feet "quiet."

The nose tackle has beaten his man and is making an inside push. You sprint out of the pocket to your right, but the defensive end has a good angle on you. Your tight end has released his block and slipped underneath. He's wide open, but the end has raised his hands and is closing in—a wall seven-feet high from his toes to his fingers.

You square your shoulders to the tight end and raise the ball to your ear. Both feet are off the ground as you move backwards and flick a pass across your body and over the defensive end, using only hips and shoulders to get anything on the ball. As you land, you're shoved onto your back with a blow to your face mask that the referee doesn't call.

When you look up, you see that your tight end has run 12 yards before a linebacker came up to tackle him. First down.

And you're doing it all over again in 30 seconds.

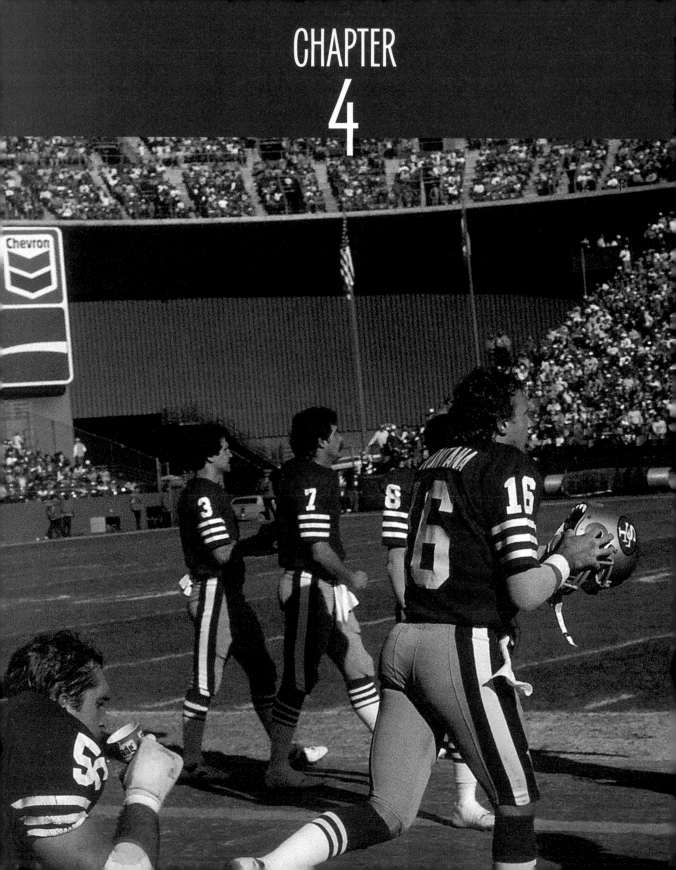

Offense is a game to be played as a unit, not as individuals. Think about it. One defensive player can make a great play, be it an end collecting a sack, a cornerback knocking down a pass, a safety making an interception, or a linebacker coming up with a run-stuffing hit. Often, these plays are the result of efforts made by other players. Still, some of these great plays can be made without any help. That is virtually impossible on offense. If the receiver makes a great play, for example, someone had to make a solid block to buy the quarterback time. The running back or tight end or guard had to pick up the blitz. The quarterback had to make the proper reads. The other receivers had to clear areas with their own routes.

THE OFFENSIVE UNIT

This unit mentality is especially important in the 49ers' system. The West Coast Offense demands that its players have patience, especially at the skill positions. These players need to understand that they won't get the ball all the time, since it gets spread around so much. I doubt any group of players could win without this team-first approach, but I *know* the 49ers couldn't.

Consider the 1981 team, which beat the Bengals in Super Bowl XVI. That team was really a bunch of no-name guys working as a unit and playing to their maximum individual capabilities. That's what the team concept is all about, especially on offense.

Look at what we had back then, coming off of 2-14, 2-14, and 6-10 seasons. We had a good front-five, though they didn't start to get voted to the Pro Bowl on a regular basis until we started winning. (Unfortunately, that's how it works. There are a lot of outstanding games played by great players which get overlooked because the teams may be struggling.) We didn't have *great* speed, though—not that anyone would

"Football is a great game, and it will teach you an awful lot. You will need to be able work with people, regardless of their color or their beliefs. You will have to be disciplined and under control at all times. It builds character, but it also reveals character. You'll learn whether you can or can't play, whether you can take that hard lick and get back up or stay down."

—Johnny Unitas,
Hall of Fame quarterback

One of the strong points of San Francisco's offensive unit was that someone always seemed to be looking out for Joe Montana.

ever admit to it at the time or even now. As a result, people underestimated us—especially our ability to find the hole and make something happen on every down. Our guys had good speed, they could get open, and they could catch the ball. That was more than enough to get the job done. The West Coast Offense doesn't require the greatest athletes—unlike, for example, the run-and-shoot, which lives and dies on speed—but it does require that these athletes understand their assignments and accept their roles. That's why we could win it all in 1981 without a 600-yard rusher and no tremendous deep threat.

TEAMMATES

It was easier to work with guys I had a relationship with—especially when things were not going as planned on the field. Don't think that the quarterback has to be closer to the receivers than to the running backs or the linemen. It should be equal. Taking the time to develop these relationships will be very helpful, especially when you're new to an offense. It'll take a few weeks before things begin to click, sometimes a month. Having people you can listen to, who are already familiar with the concepts, will lighten the burden.

Let's look at those teammates position by position.

Receivers

A quarterback must develop a good working relationship with everyone in the huddle. The receivers are extremely important, because you rely so heavily on them. The better you know them, the better your team is going to be. Often, you have to let the ball go before the receiver turns around, or before you really want to get rid of it. You really have to be on the same wavelength as them, because they'll be reading and reacting to the defense right along with you.

Wideouts (the flanker and the split end) don't need to be burners to make significant contributions. Speed is great for "stretching" the defense—making the defensive backs play well off the line of scrimmage out of fear of a deep pass—but you also like to see a guy with great hands, who can break tackles after a catch, or who isn't afraid to go over the middle. If you're really fortunate, you get all of that in one package—like I had with Jerry Rice and John Taylor.

Often, teams have two primary types of wideouts: deep threats and what they call possession receivers—the guys who run quick, precise routes, will go over the middle, and can make those tough catches in traffic for first downs. Those guys aren't always very fast. Former Oakland Raiders wide receiver and Hall of Famer Fred Biletnikoff wouldn't win too many foot races, but if he could get his hand on a ball, he was going to catch it. The same was true of Dwight Clark.

Many teams have two types of tight ends, as well. The big tight end whose primary responsibility is blocking and the quicker tight end who will pose more coverage challenges for the defense. Until about 20 years ago, most teams only had that first kind of tight end—basically a sixth offensive lineman. Then Kellen Winslow arrived and showed how dangerous a weapon a big and fast tight end could be.

"[Montana] would always tell me, 'Roger, it's just two yards. Get it.' Something positive to give me the assurance that he was on my side, encouraging me to keep the ball moving to get a first down and then set up a score. He was really good at that. He made everyone play up to another level."

—Roger Craig

"It takes awhile to get familiar with a quarterback. You have to do so many reps, over and over again. That's the one thing I really appreciated about Joe. He never got down on you. When I first came into the league and was dropping a lot of balls, he continued to throw me the ball and give me opportunities."

—Jerry Rice

Dwight Clark embraces Jerry Rice after his third quarter touchdown reception. Clark held the record for most touchdown catches by a 49er, a record that Rice would break later in his career.

Running Backs

Developing a good working relationship with running backs doesn't take as much time and effort as it does with receivers. For one thing, they're easy to understand. They just want the ball. Second, the running game comes naturally, because the quarterback only has to worry about one or two steps here or there, three at the most. Getting the ball to the tailback is especially easy. They're lined up deep, so they have a little more time to get where they need to go on a handoff. They

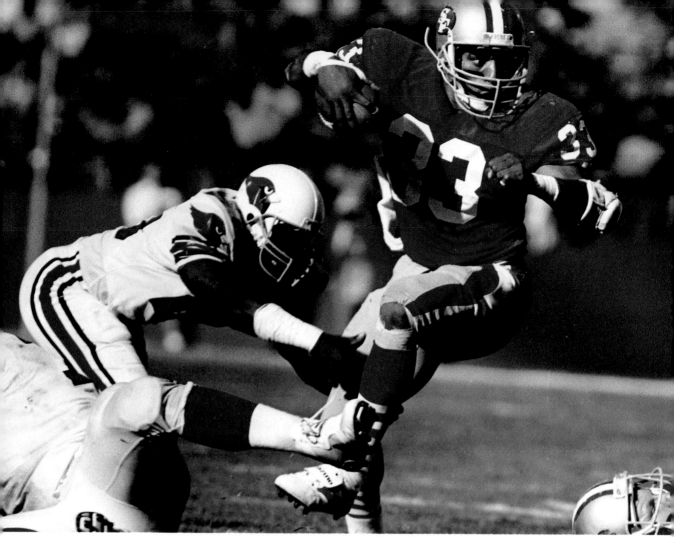

As a running back, Roger Craig led the NFL in receptions with 92 in 1985. He was also the first running back to gain 1,000 yards rushing and receiving in the same season.

figure out where you're going to be, and they get there. They're just happy to be getting the ball, the deeper in the backfield the better—since this gives them more time to find a hole.

There will be some plays which need extra work, but you'll spend a lot of time on the running game during practice—especially on the more difficult plays. Usually, that's enough for a quarterback and the running backs to get comfortable with the mechanics. If there is a continual prob-

On what a tailback needs from a quarterback: "To hand him the ball."

—*Roger Craig*

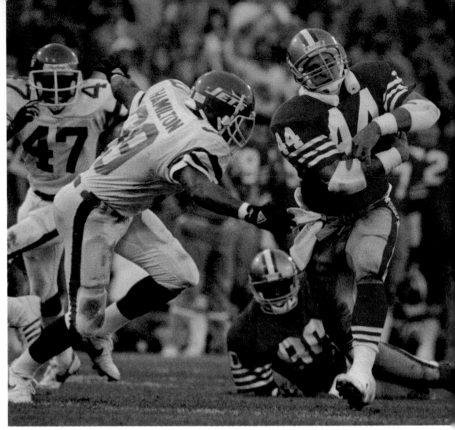

Tom Rathman was a bruising fullback who could block and catch as well as run. Here he's on his way to his first NFL touchdown.

lem, though, such as botched handoffs, you better stay after practice and fix it.

Every running back is unique, but there are three basic types: the big, bruising fullback; the little, speedy halfback; and the runner who can both outrun you and run you over.

The fullback is primarily responsible for blocking blitzing defenders on pass plays, lead-blocking for the halfback on running plays, and getting the tough yards in short yardage and goal line situations. Daryl Johnston of the Cowboys comes to mind. Every team's got one, but usually they labor in obscurity. In the West Coast Offense, fullbacks need to be good pass receivers, too. Earl Cooper and Tom Rathman in San Francisco—and Kimble Anders in Kansas City—were big guys who also happened to be excellent receivers.

The halfback, on the other hand, is often the smallest player on the field. The Giants won a Super Bowl with 5'7"

195-pound Joe Morris at halfback. One of the all-time greats, Barry Sanders, isn't much bigger. With the number of hits these halfbacks have to take during the course of a game, they may be the toughest guys, pound-for-pound, on the field. This type of halfback has the quickness to get wide, the moves to make tacklers miss, and the speed to outrun defenders when he breaks into the open field. Ricky Patton and Wendell Tyler were able to do this for us in the early-'80s.

Roger Craig is a good example of that third type of runner—the one who combines the toughness of a fullback with the agility of a halfback. Roger's added bonus was his great pass-catching ability. Ottis Anderson, of the Cardinals and Giants, is another big runner who could make you miss or go right through you. Emmitt Smith is only 5'9", but he's about as tough to bring down as Larry Csonka was. Marcus Allen isn't much bigger than me, but he may be the best short yardage runner in history—and if you want to see some moves, check out his 74-yard run in Super Bowl XVIII against the Redskins. Earl Campbell in his prime, and Bo Jackson before he got hurt, may have had the best combination of power and speed the league has seen. Then there's John Riggins—one of those rare ball carriers who could beat you to the corner or stiff-arm you so nastily he'd get called for unnecessary roughness.

Linemen

Your line takes care of you, so you need to do what you can to take care of them. A quarterback has to respect his linemen, and the linemen have to know that this respect is genuine. That means the quarterback must let the linemen know they are appreciated—since they put in a lot of work and make a lot of sacrifices without getting much attention. Check out the Super Bowl winners down through the years: some had a great running game, others had great receivers. *All* had a great line. A quarterback can't do his job without his linemen, and a team can't win without a solid front-five. As we'll talk more about later, you need to do a good job of sharing the credit.

You should do what you can to take the blame when things go wrong. For example, if the snap does get messed up, never let the center take the blame. I always had an agreement with the centers. I'd say, "Look, I'll take the blame if the ball touches the ground. When we get to the sideline, the coaches will yell at me. No big deal. But then you and I will talk about it, each saying what they thought had happened." Obviously, any center will appreciate this. You need his support and you don't want to be on the sideline battling over what happened. That's added pressure, and there's enough pressure already. It's really no big deal, anyway, since the quarterback gets most of the blame when things go wrong.

Fortunately, things have gotten better for the linemen, in terms of salary and recognition, but they still need to know that their quarterback believes in them. The ones who believe in themselves want the offense to run the ball. Pass blocking is much less aggressive than run blocking, and they want to show they can push back the guy across the line from them. After all, the defense is trying to stuff it down the offense's throat, so it makes sense that the linemen would want to do the same to them. Most of the time, linemen will want to fire out against their guys, so if you're throwing a lot, they may want to know why.

Linemen are often lumped together as just a bunch of big loads paid to get in the way of the defense, but there's a lot more to the position than that. Obviously, centers, guards, and tackles need to be strong enough to take on the big guys across the line from them. But they also need to be very agile, what with the complicated blocking schemes that are often being employed to counteract equally complicated defensive fronts and stunts. Guards, especially, need to be quick enough on their feet that they can get wide to lead the way on sweeps. Tackles need to be strong enough to take on a bull-rushing defensive end like Reggie White and agile enough to block a speed-rushing outside linebacker like Lawrence Taylor.

To handle the power, speed, and complexity of today's defenses, linemen have to rely on their brains just as much as their brawn. Not surprisingly, they aren't shy about telling you what they think is happening—and what they think they can do about it. Listen to them, because most of the time they're right. Only recently have coaches come to accept

WHERE'S THE BEEF?

The 49ers went into three of their four Super Bowls with the smaller of the two offensive lines—twice outweighed by an average of ten pounds at each position. They outgained their opponents on the ground, though—and Montana was sacked less than the opposing quarterback—all three times. The "final score": 382 yards rushing to 242, and 5 sacks allowed to 20.

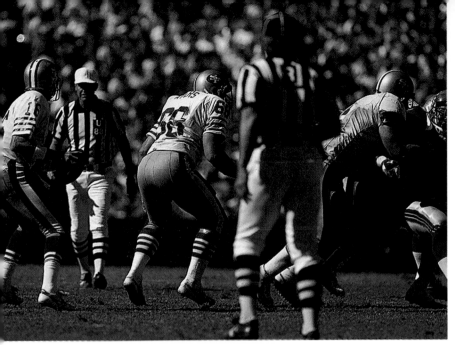

No quarterback, however talented, is going to do much without getting time to survey the defense. Here, Montana receives plenty of protection from his blockers to check out the action downfield.

what the guys up front are saying. Before, the coaching staff might keep calling the same play, over and over, to force a situation they thought was best. You can't get any closer to the action than the trenches, though, so doesn't it make sense that the linemen would know what's going on there better than anyone?

Whatever the position, talent—as some teams have found—won't cut it alone. Players—from all different backgrounds, with just as diverse personalities—need to play well together. And the quarterback will have to shoulder much of the burden of making sure that happens.

TAKING CHARGE

In the huddle, the quarterback is in charge—but you have to trust your teammates and understand the plays in order to make the plays work. Let's talk about leadership first, then get into play-calling later—because without developing your leader-ship skills, you're probably not going to get the opportunity to do much else anyway.

LEADERSHIP

There's a sign you sometimes see in football locker rooms. It says: "Good Players Inspire Themselves, Great Players Inspire Others." In my mind, the same goes for quarterbacks—good, great, or otherwise. It's not enough to be driven to succeed personally, you need to bring everyone else up with you. It's not enough to have confidence in your own abilities, you need to have the same faith in the guys around you.

The great leaders in sports—Mark Messier and Larry Bird are just two who come to mind—both had one thing in common. They made their teammates better players. Messier and Bird had different ways of doing it, both on and off the ice/court. They are both great scorers, but even better passers. Not only are they willing to do the dirty work, they revel in it—going into the corners and taking the body, or grabbing rebounds and diving for loose balls. They challenge their teammates to step it up when appropriate—or take the heat off of them by putting the pressure on themselves. Bird criticized his teammates for being soft in their first championship showdown against the Lakers, and the Celtics responded with some fierce play that turned the series around. Messier's guarantee of a victory hit the papers the morning of a crucial playoff game, serving to both restore confidence in his teammates and focus the pressure on himself. The Rangers staved off elimination that night as Messier scored three goals, and the team went on to win the series and eventually its first Stanley Cup in 54 years.

> ". . . Leaders are not born. Leaders are made, and they are made by effort and hard work."
>
> —*Vince Lombardi, legendary coach*

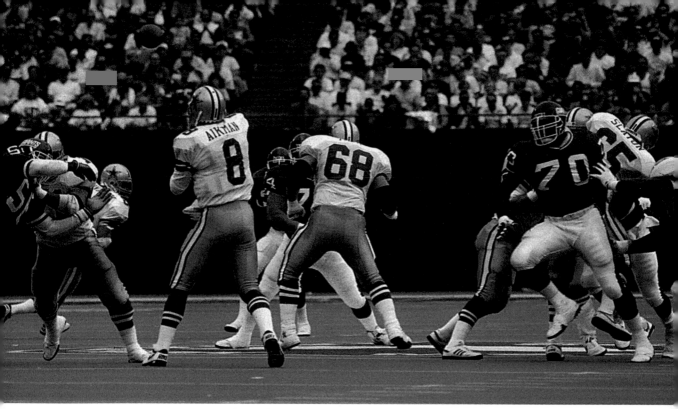

The 6'4" 230-pound frame of Dallas Cowboy Troy Aikman makes him a prototypical quarterback on the '90s, but what his size does not exhibit is his outstanding leadership on the field. Aikman helped resurrect the winning tradition in Dallas as they captured three Super Bowl championships in four years.

On the football field, I think of a guy like Bart Starr. His Packers won the first two Super Bowls and three championships prior to that. With Green Bay's balanced attack—much like Troy Aikman's Dallas Cowboys—Starr never led the league in yardage or touchdown passes. Like Aikman, he was more interested in winning games than in being a statistical leader.

If step one in being a quarterback is practice, step one in being a leader is to do your job well. Preparation is the key to that. A lot of leadership is in the details. In many ways, you're a coach on the field. The head coach will be relying on you to know where everybody is, to make sure everybody is in place. If there's a question on the field, in the huddle, at the line, or between plays, nobody is asking the running back, "Hey, what do I do on this?" You're the one who has to know.

Leading the Way

For most fans, Bart Starr's most memorable moment is his game-winning quarter-back sneak in the 1967 NFL Championship Game. Even more impressive is everything that led up to that. It was 13 degrees below zero in Green Bay for that game, with a –40 wind chill factor. Despite these frigid conditions—not to mention a fierce Cowboy defense that stuffed the Packer running game while sacking him eight times, and a passing offense that had been mediocre at best during the regular season—Starr was able to find a way to move his team through the air. Down three with 13 seconds to go, no time outs left, and the ball on the 1-yard line, he talked Vince Lombardi into calling his own number for a quarterback sneak, rather than playing it safe with a pass that, if it was incomplete, would have left them enough time to kick a tying field goal. It was his only rushing touchdown of the season.

In that huddle on the final drive, Starr exuded a calm confidence that carried over to everyone else on the offensive unit. The Cowboys were a younger team; the Packers no longer had its Hall of Fame running backs Jim Taylor and Paul Hornung; and the core of their offensive line—Forrest Gregg, Jerry Kramer, and Fuzzy Thurston—were all getting up in years. There was every reason for the Packers to figure that this might be the end of the line and give up. Starr wouldn't let them.

If you're prepared when you walk onto the field, you will be a lot more confident—and it will show. A quarterback's confidence can spread to the entire team. You don't want them wondering, "What's he going to do with the ball now?" You want them saying, "We're glad he's on our side." One of the greatest compliments any teammate ever gave me was from wide receiver Freddie Solomon. About me he said, "He always gets the job done." Your guys must have that feeling inside. In return, you have to have—and show—that same sort of confidence in them.

Here are some things to work at if you want to be a leader at quarterback.

Share the Credit

The quarterback will always receive too much credit from the media and fans when things go right and too much blame

During Montana's years with the team, the 49ers expected to score, and individual players rarely called attention to themselves when they did.

when things go wrong. There's nothing you can do about that. You shouldn't care too much about what the outsiders have to say about you, anyway. You should care a whole lot about what your teammates think. One thing that will help you build good relationships with them is to keep taking all of that blame, while doing your best to share the credit. After all, your teammates deserve it. The defense needs to get you the ball, the line needs to block for you, and the backs and receivers need to move the ball that you're delivering to them. Let them know, even if others think you did it all yourself, that *you* know it was a team effort.

If you handle the good times well, your teammates will pick you up when things are going bad for you. But if you're always throwing out your chest and screaming and yelling and telling everybody how good you are . . . well, you'll find out, as soon as the bad times come, how big a mistake that was. Not that you don't want to feel good about what you did yesterday, or have confidence or what you'll do tomorrow— all quarterbacks need that. Confidence in one's ability, though, doesn't necessarily have to translate into cockiness or arrogance.

Work Hard

Since the quarterback is often the "golden boy"—getting all the credit when things are going well—you should expect that some of your teammates might get jealous. They might even begin to think you're getting special treatment from the coaches, too. You're probably not, but in these cases, it's the perception that matters. Avoid even the *appearance* of favoritism. Work hard. Don't be the last to arrive or the first to leave. Don't skip sessions in the weight room. One good rule for a leader is not to expect anything from your teammates that you wouldn't do yourself.

Remain Calm

You've got to be the guy who keeps your teammates from getting too giddy when things are going well, and who brings them back up when things aren't going your way. You will find that your team will take on your personality. Regardless of the score, a team needs to remain calm and maintain its concentration if it is going to succeed. If you throw your helmet or pout when things aren't going well, you can't ask your teammates to keep their poise. They might not say it, but you'll lose some of their respect, too, and it will take a long time to get it back. The same goes for finger-pointing and showboating when you're winning. All you're doing is firing up the other team. Remember, you don't have to go

Just Play the Game

Here are two on-field exchanges from the 1981 NFC Championship Game between the upstart San Francisco 49ers and the less-than-respectful Dallas Cowboys.

Joe Montana to Too Tall Jones after a long pass completion: "Respect *that*!"

Offensive tackle Keith Fahnhorst: "Settle down, Joe. You're getting them worked up, and they're taking it out on me."

Harvey Martin to Joe Montana after a sack: "I will be back."

Joe Montana: "Well, I hope so, because I was beginning to think you weren't in the game."

Center Randy Cross: "Joe, shut up and just play."

one-on-one against anyone, but your teammates do—and they don't want to face a bunch of angry guys. When a quarterback tries to show up the defense, it's like a basketball player talking trash *to the guy someone else is guarding.* Your teammates will put a stop to that very quickly.

Focus on Results

When things don't go right, you're going to get blamed. There might be some very good reasons for the team's troubles that are out of control. That doesn't matter. *Don't make excuses for yourself, and don't point fingers at anyone else.* Results are what matter in football, and that's where your focus should be. Since it's winning that matters, if a teammate has a problem, *you* have a problem. Work with him on it. This results-orientation is especially important if you haven't won anything yet. Once you accomplish some things, once you've been a key part of some winning teams, you will see the power you have to positively influence your team's attitude and approach. Coach Bill Parcells calls that "having some pelts."

Montana listens on the sidelines to Notre Dame head coach Dan Devine. Part of becoming a good leader is listening and learning.

Be Yourself

None of the above should involve changing your personality. (After all, if you're selfish, lazy, or unstable, no coach is going to give you the chance to play quarterback in the first place.) It's important to be yourself. Many athletes make the mistake of trying too hard, and they end up not being themselves. That won't get it done. The last thing you want is to have people say, "That's not really him." People will see right through that. They might even think you're putting on an act just to be named captain by the coaches. If you've got a sense of humor, don't think that you can't use it. In fact, a joke at the right time could be exactly what your teammates need. If you're the strong, silent type, don't try to turn yourself into

On whether Archie
Manning would be calling
the plays for the Oilers:
"No, he'll call our plays.
We're not gonna let him
make up any."

—Bum Phillips

a cheerleader. There are plenty of stories about the quiet quarterbacks who could deliver more with a dirty look than anyone else could by screaming and yelling.

Finally, part of being yourself is *not* trying to be everyone's friend. You're never going to be the most popular guy on the team anyway—especially since part of your job will be to deliver the occasional unpleasant message—so don't even bother to try. It's respect you need, not popularity.

None of this will matter all that much if you don't believe in yourself and your team. If you don't believe you'll be successful, you probably won't be. No one can give you that feeling. It has to come from within. If you don't have it, people will know.

PLAY-CALLING

The game has changed, and quarterbacks are there not to call plays, but to execute. Quarterbacks today only call their own plays during the two-minute drills—which was fine with me. It was hard enough for me just to remember them.

"The major difference between the quarterback position today and when we played has to do with the responsibility of making the right play selection. Today, it comes from a coordinated group of people, starting with coaches in the press box. That does take a tremendous burden off the quarterback. There are some quarterbacks who are playing today that might not have been able to play in our day. Then again, there are many quarterbacks from our era who couldn't throw nearly as well as many of the passers today."

—Y.A. Tittle,
Hall of Fame quarterback

Coaches have a better feel of what to call, based on down and distance, because they study the game that way. You'd do your best to go with what they called, but there would be times in the huddle when a play would come in and, trying hard to sound convincing, you'd say, "All right, guys. Ready for this one?" Then after you'd run this play a couple of times, the call would come in again and the players would say, "Oh no! Change it! Go my way!" I played with some running backs who weren't above *begging* for the ball. It could be pretty funny. Most quarterbacks have the option of changing plays. In most cases, the coaches will want to know why. On the whole, they don't like you changing what they send in. If it works, the coach will shrug. If it doesn't, you'll get chewed out big time.

In general, you don't want to question what is coming in, especially in front of your teammates. You don't want that glimmer of doubt in their minds. They won't give everything if they believe the play isn't going to work. You have to sound confident that it will work, even if you have your doubts. Early on, you may have doubts about throwing long. I did. So when a deep pass play comes in from the sidelines, you need

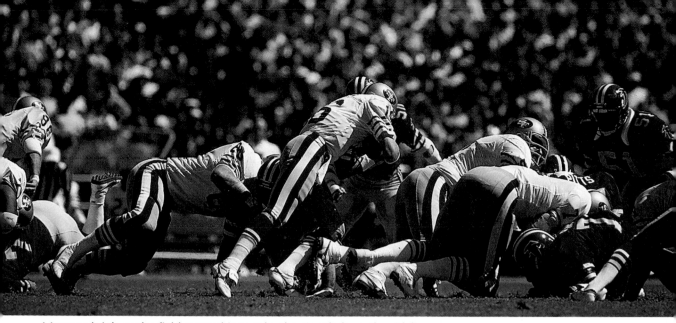

Montana's job as the field general is to take the signals from the sidelines and relay the play to rest of the team in the huddle. Joe may not have been particularly excited about the play calling on this down, but he sticks his head in there for a first down.

to do your best to sound upbeat in the huddle. You want to project a feeling of confidence to the receiver going long, even if you're feeling very tentative.

There will be those unavoidable times, though, when you get behind and everybody is going crazy—including yourself—and you'll slip up and say something negative about a play. Try not to do that. In most cases, the more confident you are about doing something, and about the projected outcome, the better off everybody feels. Including yourself, even if you don't believe it. Sometimes you can just make it happen.

Decoding the Play

The terminology each team uses for its plays is completely different, and often sounds like some kind of alien language: *pro split right counter 34*, for example. Just to show that there is a method to this madness, here is a translation of this play.

The first word indicates the offensive set, in this case a pro set—two running backs, tight end, flanker, and split end. The second word indicates the formation—*split*, meaning that the backs are lined up evenly with one another on opposite sides of the quarterback. The third word indicates where the tight

PLAY-CALLING

Paul Brown coached the Cleveland Browns during the '40s, '50s, and early-'60s, winning three NFL titles. Brown's attention to detail led him to call the plays from the sideline, and put coaches up in the booth. Brown was the first coach ever to establish that degree of control over his offense, and he was also a taskmaster and disciplinarian who could be intimidating to his players. Once, when one of Brown's "messengers" brought a play into the huddle that the quarterback didn't care for, the messenger was told to go back to the sideline and ask the coach for another one. The messenger hesitated, then said, "Go tell him yourself." Brown was not without a sense of humor, however: he occasionally sent his messenger into the huddle to tell the quarterback, "Surprise me."

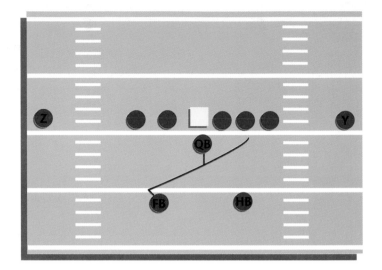

The name of this play, "pro split right counter 34," is proof quarterbacks don't simply draw their plays in the dirt. Here, the fullback gets the call, and runs the ball between the right tackle and the tight end.

end will line up; in this case, the "strong" side is the *right* side. The fourth word is the type of play being called, in this case a *counter*. This is a run where the ball carrier will take his first step one way to throw off the defense, then run in the other direction. Finally, *34* indicates who will get the ball and where he'll run it. The *3* indicates fullback—a *2* would mean the halfback, while a *1* would be the quarterback. The second digit—*4*—is the hole the fullback will be running into, in this case between the right tackle and the tight end. (*Zero* would be the hole between the center and the right guard, *1* the center and the left guard, *2* the right guard and right tackle, *3* the left guard and the left tackle, *5* off left tackle, *6* and *8* wide and wider right, *7* and *9* wide and wider left.) Pass plays are numbered from *70* to *99*, with the first digit indicating the primary receiver, and the second digit, the route.

A play from the 49ers' playbook is Red Left Slot Waggle Right X Out. "Red" is the formation, "Left" is the side on which the tight end will line up, "Slot" means two receivers on the same side (opposite the tight end), "Waggle Right" means a sprint-out to the right, and "X Out" is the pass pattern. In this case, it means that the split-end is the primary receiver (X = split end, Y = tight end, and Z = flanker), and he will run an out pattern. Other teams use three-digit numbers rather than words to describe pass patterns. Each pattern is given a number from 0 through 9, so the three digits indicate the routes to be run by the split end, tight end, and flanker.

You may play for a team that uses terminology similar to this or completely different, but, when broken down and translated, these plays will no longer appear so alien.

WHAT REALLY GOES ON IN THERE, ANYWAY?

People ask about being inside the huddle more than anything. That could be because the huddle is about the only place networks can't put a television camera and microphone these days. Much like the locker room, this is sacred ground for football players. We don't want people to know what goes on there. Words are said that aren't very pretty, and, if taken out of context, could keep the media busy for weeks. Then there is the secrecy factor. You don't want the opposition to have any clue of what might be going on in there. Ideally, working inside the huddle should be a well-controlled routine. Unfortunately, it tends to get crazy in there.

Two of my favorite huddle stories come from two of our most famous drives. The first was at the end of Super Bowl XXIII, the rematch against the Bengals. Our defense had played well that day, but our offense hadn't. Sam Wyche, the Bengals head coach (and my first quarterbacks coach in San Francisco) was all over us. The Bengals even had a read on our audibles. They knew exactly what we were going to do. At times I had to wonder whether this was going to be one of those days where nothing goes right. When that happens, it's just a matter of trying to stay close—and stay calm. With 3:10 to go, down 16-13, and the ball on our own 8-yard line, I spotted the late John Candy standing on the sideline. I pointed him out to one of our linemen, Harris Barton, who's a movie buff like myself. We laughed, realizing how absurd it was that we were paying more attention to the celebrities on the sidelines than to the game itself.

Another memorable moment in the huddle was during the drive to "The Catch" in the 1981 NFC Championship

Boomer Esiason relays the play to his teammates in the huddle. Esiason and the Bengals faced Montana and the 49ers in Super Bowl XXIII.

Game against the Cowboys—down 27-21 with the ball on our own 11 and 4:54 to go. A lot of our guys had been sick with the flu that week—including Dwight Clark and our center, Randy Cross—but they'd sucked it up and played hard all day. Then, right there, in the middle of the biggest drive of our professional careers, a chance to go to the Super Bowl hanging in the balance, I hear somebody groan and say, "What do you want to do that here for?" As it turns out, Cross had thrown up right in the huddle. Talk about focus—I hadn't even noticed.

Can you *always* be calm, cool, and collected? No. You hear about people losing it inside the huddle, and that happened to me several times—but only when a guy made a mistake time after time after time; or a guy missed a block on consecutive plays or within short periods of time; or a guy ran the wrong route in the same play a couple of times. Sometimes it's just a matter of your teammates not concentrating or paying attention. You have the right to demand their best, and sometimes, in the heat of battle, you're not polite about it.

I had plenty of great coaching in terms of throwing and footwork, but no one ever taught me how to act inside the huddle. It's just one of those things I had to figure out over the years. These stories just point out two of the things I tried to be—calm and focused. You also need to be encouraging, especially when things aren't going well. It's still supposed to be a game, which means it should be fun. Every player makes mistakes. The worst thing that can happen is having someone make a great play and someone else mess up and ruin the whole effort—a missed block, a botched assignment while running a route, or a penalty during a big gain. Sure, it's frustrating, but you're in this together. Since you're on the field when those mistakes occur, there's no one there to help out except for the guys in the huddle. Think about it. Let's say you're coming back to the huddle, and you're down because you've made an honest mistake. How would you feel if one of your teammates started screaming at you? No one likes that—besides, you get plenty of it from the coaches once you get to the sideline.

There is no one right way to be a leader. It goes back to being yourself. You don't want to be fighting yourselves when you should have been taking on the other team. My style was to be encouraging most of the time. My teammates were professional enough that they knew when they'd made a mistake, and they'd come back to the huddle apologizing for it. Chances are, the lineman who missed a block on a sack will feel worse than you did, so tell him not to worry about it.

Only on rare occasions did I chew someone out. You need to be certain that you do it before someone else decides to, though. If a player keeps making the same mistake, over and over, the quarterback should be the one to say something, not the tailback or right tackle. The player making the mistakes can take that kind of criticism a lot easier from the quarterback. Most guys will recognize that that's part of your role.

Players often key off the attitude of their quarterback. With that in mind, the quarterback needs to be well-prepared and focused, but should stay loose and upbeat. Maintaining a positive attitude was never too difficult for Montana. His career gave him a lot to smile about.

There are a lot of ways to deliver a message without being overly confrontational. Even when you're getting on somebody, you can do it in a way that will build him up. "Come on, you're better than that." "How can you let a guy like that beat you? He can't carry your helmet." Stuff like that. You're showing respect for him at the same time you're delivering a message. Now, I remember hearing about Jim McMahon, quarterback of the Chicago Bears, kicking one of his linemen in the butt on the way to the line of scrimmage. McMahon was crazy enough to get away with that kind of thing, and his lineman responded by taking it out on the guy across from him. That wasn't my style, and I sure wouldn't recommend it, but Jim was a big winner in the NFL before his shoulder got wrecked on a late hit. He just had his own way of doing things.

You also have to be willing to defuse situations in which someone starts getting on *you*—for example, if a receiver comes back to the huddle yelling at you and demanding the ball. Inside, you're thinking, "You come in here yelling at me and now you want me to do something for you? I don't think so." What you need to do, though, is: 1) not hold a grudge against him, because that's going to hurt the team; and 2) let him know that screaming and yelling for the ball is not how you do business. Even if he's your best receiver, you can't back down. You're in charge.

Even though you're in charge, don't think of yourself as the chairman of the board inside the huddle—that you're the brains of the operation and everyone else is your supporting cast. It's more like you're the office manager. You've got to make sure everyone is doing his job properly—and is happy and enjoying what he is doing. Otherwise, production falls off.

Whether you're being cool, funny, encouraging, or tough, it's all intended to keep everyone "up" and trying to play their best. As you can see, it's not always the rah-rah stuff that works. Sometimes it's just the little things you do to make people laugh and relax. Remember, offense is like a chain reaction. If you're going to throw a pass or run the ball, there has to be a hole. The linemen need to block their marked opponents. The receivers have to catch the ball, or the runners have to find the hole. Anything and everything can happen, and it takes all the players on the field to execute. In some cases, the quarterback may be the least important guy out there, because all he may do is hand the ball off and get out of the way. You need everyone working together. You can't have one guy down on himself when he may be blocking for the guy who's getting the ball.

In the huddle, you need to get your team to work together. Confidence and leadership are the keys to making that happen.

AT THE LINE

Much of the really crucial stuff that's going on in a football game is hidden from the fans. They wait impatiently between plays for the next snap and the ensuing action, but what goes on from the time the quarterback breaks the huddle to the moment the ball is snapped can determine the outcome of a game just as much as a great catch or a goal line stand.

That's right, many games are won and lost while the ball isn't even in play. A large chunk of a quarterback's contribution is made during those 15 seconds that he's walking to the line and standing under center. NFL quarterbacks may not be calling their own plays anymore, but they have a new responsibility that wasn't nearly so complicated 20 or 30 years ago: reading the defense. Do it right and your offense looks unstoppable. Do it wrong and your unit looks hopelessly overmatched.

DEFENSE 101

Every team will do things a little bit differently, but basically, there are three variables to defense: formation, coverage, and pass rush.

Formation

There have been 11 men on defense for the 75+ years that the NFL has been in existence, but coaches have found seemingly endless ways to line these guys up. The four most common formations today are 3-4, 4-3, nickel, and dime. The 3-4 features three defensive linemen (a nose tackle and two ends), four linebackers (two outside and two inside), and four defensive backs (two safeties and two cornerbacks). The 4-3 features four defensive linemen (two tackles and two ends), three linebackers, and four defensive backs. The nickel features five defensive backs, and it can be played with three linemen and three linebackers, or four linemen and two linebackers. The dime features six defensive backs, and it can be

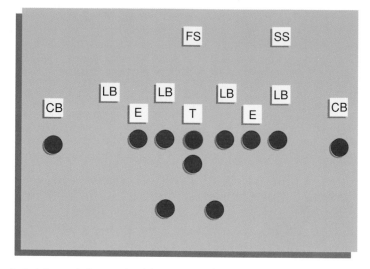

The 3-4 defense is best suited for a team that has quick and agile linebackers as well as a strong nose tackle. Because there are only three men on the front line, the nose tackle is the key to stopping the run up the middle.

THE 3-4 DEFENSE

No scheme is "the best." It all depends on down, distance, score, time, conditions, you name it. Sometimes it depends on personnel. Bum Phillips, coach of the Houston Oilers, was credited with bringing the 3-4 to the NFL from the NCAA in the mid-'70s. His reason for doing so? Bum maintained that it was simply a matter of having more good linebackers than linemen.

played with four linemen and one linebacker, or three linemen and two linebackers.

Each formation has its strengths and weaknesses. By replacing a defensive tackle with a linebacker in the 3-4, you're putting more speed on the field while losing some beef up front. That's why a big, strong nose tackle is vital to making the 3-4 work. Without him, it will be very tough for this scheme to consistently stop the run up the middle, but a strong nose tackle and a speed rusher at outside linebacker (Jim Burt and Lawrence Taylor of the Giants' first Super Bowl team come to mind) can make this a very difficult defense to move the ball against. The 4-3 gives you more beef up front, but it used to make it more difficult to allow an outside linebacker to blitz frequently the way LT used to. Now teams are blitzing linebackers out of this formation, while dropping linemen into coverage—simply because these defenders are good enough athletes to do that. Teams are sending anyone from anywhere at any time without worrying so much about being "sound" in coverage. They're doing just about anything to confuse the quarterback as he tries to read the defense, an approach that brought Buddy Ryan a lot of success.

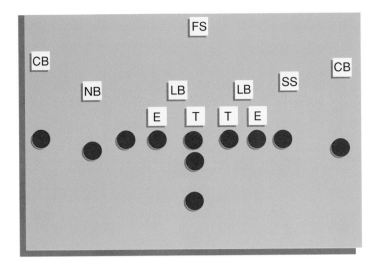

The nickel defense was originally used late in the game or in third down, long-yardage situations. It is now used by teams more frequently to counter offenses which use three, four, or even five wideouts.

The nickel and dime are used in long-yardage situations, or against teams that use three, four, or even five wideouts. You're taking muscle off the field and replacing it with speed, so these formations will yield some big runs if the offense chooses to go that way. You also end up trading some pass rush for better coverage. If these defensive backs do their jobs, a nickel or dime package can end up with what is called a "coverage sack," as the linemen finally get to the quarterback simply because he has no open receivers.

Coverage

Most of the time in the pros, you'll see zone coverage, as opposed to man-to-man, simply because the receivers are too good for most cornerbacks to be able to stay with them. In most zone defenses, defenders are responsible for seven areas on the field. These areas are the left and right "flats" (the line of scrimmage to about 10 yards deep), "underneath" (in between the flats and behind the defensive line), left and right "short" (about 10 to 20 yards deep), and the two deep areas that are usually covered by the safeties.

Again, there are strengths and weaknesses to each approach. If the corners can play solid man-to-man defense

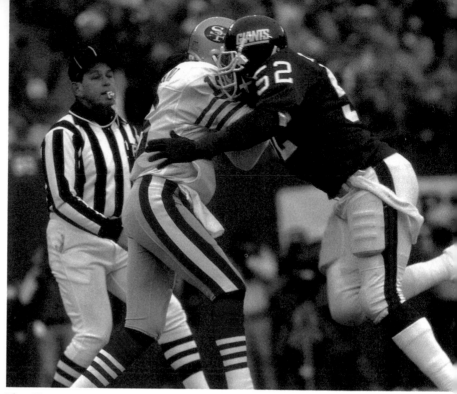

The Giants were able to play a defense that dared Montana to throw long, clogged up the short and underneath passing lanes, yet still mounted a pass rush. Linebackers like Pepper Johnson, above, as well as Lawrence Taylor, Carl Banks, and Harry Carson, had a lot to do with that.

> "Great corners . . . can control what an offense does, just by their presence. They can force an offense to avoid a huge chunk of the field."
>
> —*Ernest Givins, wide receiver*

against the wideouts, and the strong safety can handle the tight end, that frees up more defenders to rush the quarterback. If the corners *can't* handle these receivers in man-to-man coverage, the offense will make some big plays, even in the face of a stiff pass rush. In general, zone defense is a more conservative, bend-but-don't-break approach where coverage is increased while pressure on the quarterback is lessened.

You may also see combinations of man and zone coverage. Defenses are a lot more complicated than they used to be, which is another reason why play-calling has been taken over by the coach. The quarterback has enough to think about just trying to figure out what the other 11 guys are doing.

Pass Rush

The final variable is the number of defenders that will be coming after the quarterback. Nearly 100% of the time, you will be seeing at least three rushers. The big question is whether the linebackers or safeties will be blitzing and, if so, how many. It used to be that a blitz meant man-to-man coverage, although defenses have begun to blitz out of the zone, too. They are exposing an area of the field to the quarterback in order to gain the element of surprise. Offenses will eventually figure out how to pick up the zone blitz consistently and exploit it—by keeping the running backs in on protection and counting on the wideouts to get open—but it's a pretty effective defensive ploy at the moment because it's messing up the quarterback's ability to read the defense.

Even these three basic variables—formation, coverage, and pass rush—can get complicated fairly quickly when you throw them all together. A play that will work quite nicely against a 3-4, two-deep zone with no blitz won't do much against a 4-3, man-to-man with a safety blitz. If you think that's confusing, just keep reading. When I first came into the league, I could read some defenses just by looking at the defensive front. Not anymore.

READING THE DEFENSE

Defenses may have been less sophisticated in the past, but they have always had one thing in common: trying to hide things from the quarterback. In most cases, though, you can always tell, right at the snap of the ball, what is going to happen. Here is basically what I did:

1. check the linemen for the defensive front;

2. check the safeties for the coverage;

3. check the cornerbacks for some possible quirks in the coverage;

4. check the linebackers—especially the outside linebackers—for a possible blitz.

That's an oversimplification, but it's pretty accurate. If the play is called for a running back or the tight end, you'll probably be tempted to look at the linebackers first. Don't. Look at all the defenders, and try to do it in the same order with the same emphasis.

"There was a philosophy in the game at one time that said defense was a game of reaction. . . . Defenses would sit there and read the offenses and their blocking patterns as they came. If you do that, you give the offense the edge, and you have to be a super kind of athlete to defeat it. [Now you need to] attack the offense at the snap of the ball."

—*Chuck Noll*

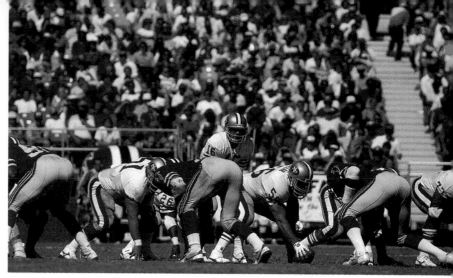

Montana checks out the defense in attempt to anticipate their coverage. As a quarterback, you have to read the defensive scheme before the play clock runs out—and do so without tipping off the defense what your unit is planning to do with the ball.

The Linemen

As you break the huddle, you should be checking the defensive linemen to see how they are lined up, either as a four-man or three-man front. The three-man is easier to spot, because it rarely changes. A four-man line, in contrast, sometimes causes a quarterback to change the call at the line. There is a basic 4-3 look, and then there is a look where the strong-side (the side of the field where the tight end is lined up) linebacker moves inside and the defensive end slides out over the tight end. We called that a 47. If the weak-side linebacker moved in and the defensive end slid out, that was a 45. In addition to these adjustments, the linemen may start sliding along the line, shifting so that the line was stacked more to the strong-side or weak-side. That's when you see the offensive linemen pointing and talking to one another; they're changing their blocking assignments. This was one of the reasons the 1985 Bears defense was so devastating. The offensive linemen hadn't figured out yet how to block it. Plenty of quarterbacks had wide open receivers against the Bears, but they weren't able to remain standing long enough to complete the pass.

These shifts were what we called "overs" and "unders." A "pure over" called for both linebackers to play on the line of scrimmage, outside of the ends, with the middle linebacker over the weak-side guard. Meanwhile, the weak-side defensive tackle moves over to the nose to play in front of the center. A "pure under" would mean that the middle linebacker was over the strong-side guard. This all has to be recognized by the quarterback at the line of scrimmage, preferably before he gets under center. From there, he needs to read the pass coverage. That's the most important read for a quarterback.

The Safeties

Nothing is more important to reading the defense than the safeties. You should check the weak-side (free) safety first. If he goes back to the middle of the field, it will be some kind of zone—either a three-deep zone or some type of zone coverage with a little man-to-man. It won't be a two-deep zone, because he would play to the left or right in that scheme, not in the middle. So if he goes to the middle of the field, you should next look to the strong safety. (Sometimes you can see them both at the same time.) If the strong safety moves forward, then to the outside, it's probably a three-deep zone. Since the corners and the free safety will be responsible for the deep areas in a three-deep zone, the strong safety is coming forward and to the outside to take one of the short areas.

Underneath the deep areas in a three-deep zone, there are usually four other defensive players with coverage responsibilities. Typically, an outside linebacker and the strong safety cover the flats. The other linebackers are responsible for anything underneath. In a two-deep zone, the safeties are responsible for the deep areas. Three linebackers tend to drop into underneath coverage, while the corners may play man-to-man on the wideouts.

The two-deep and three-deep zones I've described are fairly easy reads. That's why defenses today have begun to switch or camouflage formations with movement at the line of scrimmage. The goal is to make the offense think zone coverage is man-to-man. A cornerback and strong safety might switch positions or a linebacker and the strong safety might line up on top of the tight end. A linebacker and the strong safety might switch positions, with the strong safety responsible for one of the flats. A defense can get a lot of interceptions by tricking a quarterback into thinking he's throwing into man-to-man coverage.

So you not only need to read the defense, you need to study enough film that you can begin to recognize the tricks,

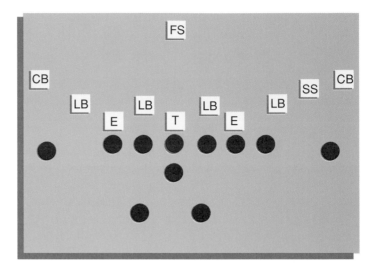

In a three-deep zone, the free safety will be positioned in the middle of the field. The strong safety will move forward and to the outside to cover one of the short areas.

too. Some of this was taught to me in high school, but it was Sam Wyche who really taught me most of the intricacies of reading coverages and everything that goes with it.

Remember, it's the safeties who give away most of the coverages. They may move after you look at them the first time, so you should go back and look at them again before the ball is snapped.

The Cornerbacks

After reading the safeties, the quarterback should read the cornerbacks. Sometimes you can even pick up man-to-man coverage from the corners faster than the safeties. A quarterback might be able to read what the coverage is just by studying how the corners line up. In man-to-man, the cornerbacks usually line up a bit more inside. Sometimes it'll only be half a step, or even a shade. They're protecting against those crossing patterns and slants. Think about it. If it's a zone, and the receiver cuts across the middle, he'll be moving from one area to another, and the corner will simply pass him off to the defender responsible for that area. If it's man, the corner is responsible for chasing him all the way across the field. The corner will give him a step on the outside, because

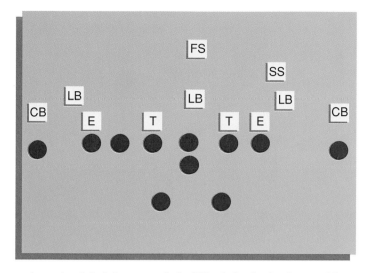

At one time, the 4-3 defense made it difficult for linebackers to blitz. Now, linemen are quick and agile, and can drop into coverage, allowing linebackers to rush the quarterback.

it's harder for the receiver to run away from him; the sideline will help him defend. The key is for a quarterback to become accustomed to seeing this slight movement in the way the cornerback lines up.

The Linebackers

Linebackers, on the other hand, are like machines in pass coverage. They go to a point, then drop straight to another point. Once the ball is snapped, the linebackers either come up toward the line, or they turn and run. When they turn and run, they are simply looking for a spot where they were told to be during practice, where they dropped in drills a thousand times. If somebody comes into that area, a linebacker will try to cover him. The advantage for a quarterback here is to try to get the ball between the linebackers—what is called a "seam" in the zone.

For a lot of linebackers, their hearts just aren't in pass coverage. They want to rush the quarterback. You can often tell that just by looking at them. John Madden often talks about "linebacker eyes" to describe that crazy look those guys can get. I did my best not to look at a linebacker's eyes. A lot of linebackers will try to look into the quarterback's eyes,

On looking quarterbacks in the eyes: "Joe was so tuned in . . . you didn't worry about Montana, because he was going to get you. But if you could eliminate other people, then you were okay."

—Matt Millen, former linebacker

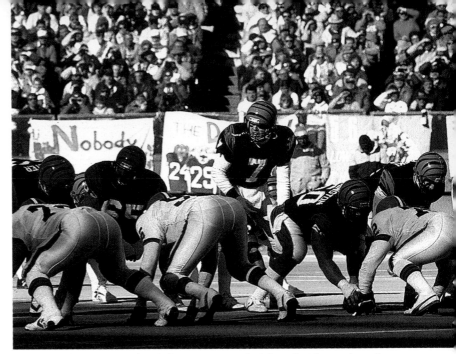

Boomer Esiason scans the defense to get a feel for what is coming. Sometimes, the hungrier a linebacker looks, the more likely he will be coming in on a blitz.

though. They're trying to psych you out. They feel they can get a read by where you're looking, figuring that's where you'll throw the ball. That's why when you're dropping back you want to keep your head looking downfield as long as possible. That way it looks the same no matter where you're going to throw. That's the quarterback's version of a poker face.

Just like one step here or there from a corner can tip you off to man-to-man coverage, one step from a linebacker can tell you a blitz is coming. Sometimes, for instance, you'll see a linebacker, especially an outside linebacker, line up on the tight end. If he takes a step outside, that usually means he's blitzing. He wants to cut down the tight end's blocking angle so that he can get a cleaner shot at the quarterback. If he's got coverage responsibility for the flat, he may also cheat a step to the outside—but more likely he'll stay on the tight end, because he wants to stick him coming off the line before he slides over to the flat. If the outside linebacker takes a step back from the line before you snap the ball, you can pretty much count on him turning and running into coverage as soon as the ball is snapped. Sometimes it won't be a step

Carl Banks is lined up wide, possibly showing blitz. The quarterback should already know he may have pressure coming from his right side.

inside or outside, but the stance of his feet, that can tell you whether he plans to blitz—or it can be as simple as the presence of a "designated blitzer," a linebacker who comes in mostly in passing situations, usually to blitz.

The actual time it takes a quarterback to pick up a blitz varies on the situation and also from passer to passer. You must be able to detect it during the first two steps after taking the ball from center, though—if you haven't already recognized it at the line.

CALLING AUDIBLES

As the quarterback stands under center, he shouldn't just be looking at what the defense is trying to do. It's not enough just to avoid a defense's strengths. More importantly, you should be thinking about the vulnerabilities the defense will be exposing. You have to have the right attitude about it; when a defense focuses on stopping one thing, they are opening up something else. It isn't pleasant to stare down the barrel of an all-out blitz, but probably no other defensive scheme offers more opportunity for a big play. Jerry Rice scored five touchdowns against the Falcons when we were facing a lot of heavy blitzes. That's how you put pressure on the defense—you identify the weak spots and holes and exploit them. If you can read the coverage and rush that the defense is showing, you can decide how and where to attack the defense.

These weak spots aren't so much with the personnel as they are with the coverages. There are always little holes in the defense where you can find a place to attack—basically because a football field is a pretty big place. Also, your guys know where they're going, but the defense doesn't. If it's a zone, you want to try to overload or "flood" one of these areas so that someone will be open regardless of the intricate, sometimes smothering coverages. We liked to catch a linebacker turned around, for instance, while he was trying to cover a tight end, by putting a running back in the same area underneath the coverage. If the linebacker knows that's coming, you'll need to throw the ball to the back's opposite shoulder to tell him which way to turn to avoid him. If the linebacker is coming in from the right, hit him in the left shoulder. If he's coming in from the left, hit him in the right shoulder. For just this reason, Bill Walsh wanted us to hit receivers in the left or right number on short passes—something the quarterbacks heard about *a lot* in practice.

You'll get some help from your receivers in reading the defense. The cues you get might not always be verbal. Receivers will touch their shirt or another part of their uniform to tell you they're going to break off their pattern and run a quick out, for example.

Audibles follow the same basic concept. These are plays that can be called at the line of scrimmage to take advantage of a weakness seen in the particular defense—if the play you've already called won't do the trick. On some teams, each audible will have a number. Each week, there will be a word or color that the quarterback will use at the line of scrimmage to indicate whether he's calling an audible. When the quarterback yells, "Yellow 52," it doesn't mean anything unless "Yellow" is that week's "hot" word. If it is, then everyone on the offense better have prepared enough to immediately know which play "52" indicates.

Sometimes a quarterback will say "Check with me" in the

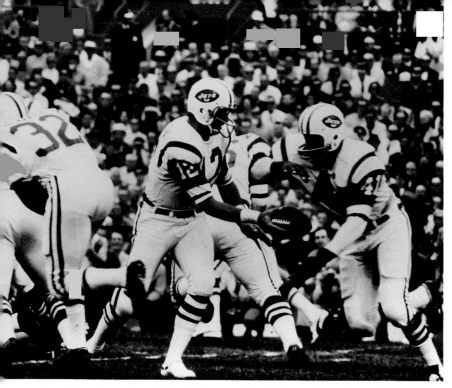

Joe Namath confused the Baltimore Colt defense throughout their 16-7 upset victory in Super Bowl III. Namath frequently waited to see how the Baltimore defense was set up before calling the play at the line of scrimmage.

huddle, which means that he'll be calling the play at the line. This is what Joe Namath did for most of the Jets' plays during Super Bowl III. With San Francisco, I would have needed a wrist band up to my shoulder to write them all down.

I didn't call many audibles with the 49ers. I didn't have a "menu" to choose from, but rather a specific play to call—if we were looking at a strong-side blitz, for example. These plays would change from week to week, depending on the strengths and weaknesses of the team we were playing. We also had a standard play to call if the play didn't come in from the sidelines in time.

If the defense thinks you're calling an audible, they might move around to try to confuse you. They might even do what middle linebacker Matt Millen did when I called, "Black 3 24 Omaha." He threw up his hands and yelled, "Oh, no! *Not* Black 3 24 Omaha!" It was pretty hard not to laugh.

One of my favorite "audibles" in San Francisco came

> "When you do call an audible, make sure it works."
>
> —*Otto Graham's advice to a young quarterback*

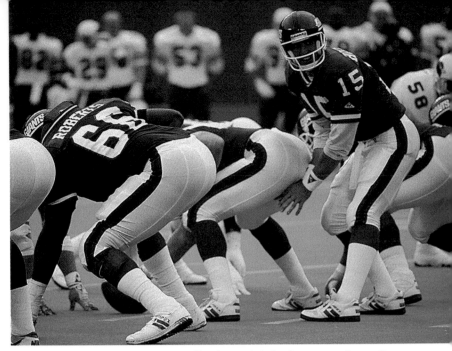
Always check to make sure your offensive unit is in the proper formation. If there is a mix-up, it could prove to be disastrous.

against the Jets in 1980. Steve DeBerg was still the starting quarterback, but Bill Walsh was finding ways to work me into the games. Steve drives us down to the 5-yard line, then runs to the sideline as if he's got a problem with his equipment. The Jets didn't know it, but this was all pre-arranged. Because I was a bit more mobile than Steve, Bill wanted me in there to surprise the defense with a quarterback bootleg. It worked.

While you're at the line checking out the defense, the defensive captain (usually the middle linebacker or one of the inside linebackers) is checking out your side of the ball and may be calling out some changes of his own. What you're showing them may be a bigger concern than what they're showing you. If you sense any confusion in the defense, get the action started as soon as your guys are set.

You get things started with the snap count, which you call in the huddle. "On one" means that the ball will be snapped on your first "hut," while "on two" means your second "hut," and so on. You can go with what's called a "rhythmic" count, where you call out the count quickly and easily: "hut, hut, hut." If you want to try to draw the defense offsides, you can go with a "hard count" where you alter the timing of your signals: "hut, hut, . . . hut," for example.

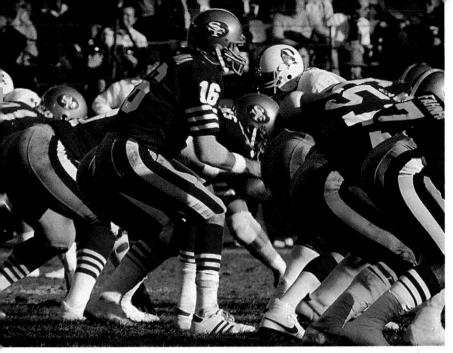

There are different snap counts a quarterback can use to keep the defense guessing. He can call a rhythmic count, a non-rhythmic (hard count) to draw the defense offsides, and a quick count (going on first sound) to try to catch the defense on their heels.

Game Footage

Your right tackle just got bull-rushed by the defensive end, and it took a great pump fake on your part just to get him off of his feet and buy the time to scramble back to the line of scrimmage. You didn't slide feet first—you were still looking for a receiver, so it was open season on you. Their left outside line-backer buried his helmet in your ribs and told you, "Not today," as he took you down. You pop right back up—not just because you don't want him to know that it hurt, but because you've only got 30 seconds before you have to do it all over again.

The referees place the ball, and the play clock starts counting down from 30. You check the down and distance—second-and-ten at their 25. You head to the center of the field at the 35, where you're met by the rest of your guys and the offensive substitutions. You're getting the plays through a transmitter in your helmet, but it's a really loud, hostile crowd, and you're in toward the closed end of their stadium. You have to hold your hands over your earholes to hear the play. They have to repeat it, which chews up a few precious seconds.

You don't have to decode the play—how the offense will line up, what patterns the receivers will run, the running backs' assignments, and the primary receiver—because you've run it so many times in practice and you've studied your playbook enough that a picture of it immediately forms in your mind. It's a pass play off a 5-step drop, with your flanker, the primary receiver, lined up right and running a square out. Your split end is lined up left, where he'll be running a streak to the end zone, then moving along the back line to the right if you get flushed out of the pocket to your right. Your tight end is lined up right, where he'll be blocking either a blitzing outside linebacker or helping out on the defensive end before releasing underneath. Your backs will line up in the I-formation. The halfback will run a weak-side comeback route that will take him to the 10-yard line and then bring him back toward the first down marker. Your fullback will be in on weak-side pass protection, then release on a swing pattern to the left as a safety valve.

You crouch down in the huddle. You repeat the play, looking your teammates in the eye, speaking distinctly so that everyone gets it, including the snap count you've chosen. You're going with a rhythmic count on three. Your fullback is a rookie and doesn't know his assignment, so you have to tell him, which costs you a few more seconds. You clap your hands to break the huddle.

You walk to the line, visualizing the play you'll be running. You're checking out the defensive personnel and the initial formation the defensive front is showing you. Then you notice that your left guard is holding two fingers behind his back. He's forgotten the snap count, and he's asking if it's two. You say, "No." He shows three fingers and you say, "Got it."

You check the play clock in the end zone—ten seconds left, barely enough. You check out your own unit to make sure they're all lined up correctly. You give your linemen time to call out their blocking assignments while you scan the defense. You know where the play is intended to go, but you make certain not to stare at that part of the field. They're in a 3-4 with four defensive backs. They've shown you 3-4 on second-and-long all day, playing man-to-man and frequently blitzing as many as three linebackers out of it. Since you're getting close to the red zone, a blitz is even more likely. With a lot less field to cover and therefore less to fear from a big play, the defense tends to take more risks. They trade some coverage for a better pass rush. But you've been reading their blitzes, beating them for big gains twice already today when you were down in close—so they may have made a halftime adjustment and be playing zone here.

You check out the cornerbacks' helmets and see the stripe down the middle. They're looking at you, and that means zone. The safeties have a lot of ground to cover and not much room to play around, so how they're lined up may give away the defensive set. The free safety is deep, shading a bit to the weak side, and the strong safety is back about 15 yards. With the cornerbacks up close to the flanker and split end, it looks like the safeties will be responsible for everything about 20 yards deep. If it's indeed the two-deep zone they've been showing you all day, the corners will be in man coverage on your wideouts, and the two inside linebackers will drop into underneath coverage. You check the weak-side inside linebacker and, sure enough, he's cheated one step back from the line, so he can drop back more quickly into coverage.

If your primary receiver doesn't run a good square out pattern, or if the corner reads the play, it'll get picked off and taken all the way. You've got to be sure about that one before you throw it.

You like the split end's streak pattern on man-to-man coverage, because he can beat the corner by five yards on that route. One of the deep safeties will be picking him up, though, unless they both bite on shorter patterns. You'll watch for that.

Your tight end could be open underneath, if he can split the seam between the linebackers. If they send one of their inside linebackers on a blitz, a short dump over the middle could get you an easy first down. If all else fails, you're pretty confident your fullback will be wide open on that swing pattern.

You think this play can work, so there's no need for an audible. The words you're yelling—"Red 36! Red 36!"—once to the left, once to the right, don't mean anything. That day's "hot" color had been red, but you changed it to blue at halftime, because you thought the defense might have read your last audible near the end of the second quarter.

Three seconds to go on the play clock.

"Hut! Hut! Hut!"

WHAT IT TAKES

My dad had always been a real sports lover, but he never tried to push me into any sport. He just gave me one piece of advice: Whatever you do, you should want to be the best. I've learned that to be the best, you need to be willing to do what it takes: to put in the time and energy to prepare yourself, to be able to handle adversity, and to have fun doing it. If any of that is missing, you should probably try something else.

PREPARATION

Scared off yet? When someone asks me what to tell a young, aspiring quarterback, I usually say, "Play golf."

After "golf," the next word out of my mouth is "practice." No short cut around that. You can never be too in shape. You can never be accurate enough, because you can never perfect the art of throwing to someone who is moving. You can never study enough film, and you can never go over your playbook pages too much. If you're tougher, smarter, and better conditioned than your opponents, you're not going to lose very often—even if they do happen to be bigger or faster than your squad. It won't come easy—but nothing worthwhile ever does.

The Practice Field

You really have only one goal when you're on the practice field. To walk off it a better player than you were when you got there. That means taking it seriously and addressing your weaknesses. If you don't like your coach pointing out these deficiencies to you, then be aware of them yourself. Work on them before he has to tell you about them. Remember that all coaches are different in how they go about their business, but they all want you to improve as a player. Some just express that a bit louder and a bit more colorfully than others.

"Basically, we look for a quarterback who can come in and compete at the highest level. Hopefully, first of all, he's a good student and can get into school and can graduate. Other than that, we look for leadership ability, skills as far as communicating with everyone, basically being a good person. And, obviously, the ability to throw the ball and make quick decisions."

—*Steve Spurrier, University of Florida coach and Heisman Trophy quarterback*

"If you're lucky enough to find a guy with a lot of head and a lot of heart, he's never going to come off the field second."

—*Vince Lombardi*

A very rare sight: Jerry Rice taking a break during a pre-season workout.

A quarterback can't be thin-skinned when it comes to criticism. Coaches will be more forceful with you than with other position players—they know what is riding on the quarterback's actions every time he touches the ball. Other positions don't have that responsibility, which begins with simply telling everyone what to do. That's why practice is so important—not just to work on your game, but to set the tone for your teammates.

Any notion that athletes don't take practice seriously—the successful ones, anyway—is a myth. Just watch Jerry Rice running hills if you don't believe me. He's one of the hardest-working athletes I've ever seen. As for me, it was on the practice field that I learned how to throw on the run. This is also where I developed "touch" on my passes. I never had the strongest arm or the tightest spiral, so I had to put in a lot of practice time to develop the consistent accuracy I needed to succeed.

The chemistry I developed with receivers like Dwight Clark, Freddie Solomon, Jerry Rice, and John Taylor began on the practice field, too. For example, getting comfortable throwing to them before they turned, so that they could catch it on the break, took a lot of hard work. Unfortunately, it's difficult to get as much time as you need with a receiver during practice. The only time a quarterback and receiver can work on certain aspects together—like Ken Stabler and Dave Casper—is after practice. You can't do it before, because the guys don't want to get tired out. Most receivers don't mind staying late though. They know that running routes for you will help them, too.

Extensive repetition is probably more important for a quarterback than for any other player. You need to get to the point where your footwork and throwing motion comes instinctively—like a free throw for Larry Bird, or Ken Griffey taking a cut at a fastball. You have to do the reps. Throwing a football with accuracy at a moving target over and through your offensive line and their pass rush is hard enough, but consider that you can't take your time because you've only got about two seconds to decide where to throw.

Ironically, taking your time is the best way to begin. Work on the fundamentals slowly—walk through them if you have to—then work on improving your quickness each day. As for

It takes much more than just a strong arm to be a quarterback. Being willing to practice and study hard to prepare for games is critical, too.

finding your receivers and deciding where to throw, that's something else that will come slowly, day by day—if you put in the effort.

But that won't come without a lot of attention paid to the mental aspect of the game.

The Mental Game

I think the mental aspect is 75% of the game for the quarterback. That's right, I think the mental is far more important than the physical. It came down to one thing: preparation.

All football players make sacrifices on the practice field and in the weight room, but there is a lot of time and energy

Practice, Practice

Two of the most famous passing combinations in NFL history are Johnny Unitas to Raymond Berry and Ken Stabler to Dave Casper. This didn't happen by accident.

Berry was Unitas's "money" receiver. He didn't have great speed, but his hands were legendary. The Baltimore Colts had a drill that helped Berry develop his uncanny pass-catching abilities. He would stand with his back to Unitas. Unitas would throw a ball, a coach would yell for Berry to turn, and Berry would then spin to face the quarterback. In a split second, he would find the ball—high, low, in, out—and catch it, often one-handed.

Casper was the guy Stabler looked to when the game was on the line. When the Raiders got inside the 15-yard line, Stabler would take a short drop and loft a high pass to his tight end in the corner of the end zone. If they were on the money, it couldn't be stopped. Stabler and Casper usually were, because they ran the play about 25 times at the end of each practice. In fact, they won one of the greatest football games ever played on this play—37-31 in double overtime in the playoffs against the Baltimore Colts on Christmas Eve 1977.

> "The one with the coolest head survives. The one with the coolest head wins. Joe's cool-headed because he prepares."
>
> —Boomer Esiason, quarterback

invested by players, especially quarterbacks, *off* the field. Studying is essential. If you watch Marino, Favre, Aikman, or Elway on television, and you think they're just drawing plays in the dirt or making it up as they go along, forget it. If you don't prepare, you'll pay for it. More often than not, you'll let down your teammates, embarrass yourself, and maybe even get hurt. There have been times when I thought I'd prepared enough, only to get into the game and be unable to remember all the formations. Needless to say, those were rough games.

In addition to knowing your own offense inside and out, you have to know the defense you are going to see—so you can react quickly. That way, you're not going to say to yourself, "Now let me see, that's a two-deep-zone-man-underneath"—which in football-speak means linebackers coming out of a 3-4 defense. You don't want to stop and think about that. It's got to be a natural reaction. You have to detect the formation at the line and call an audible if necessary. Once

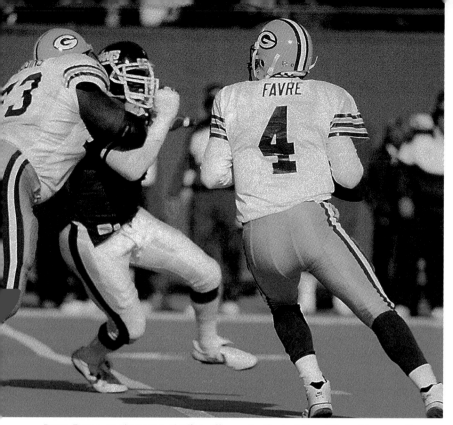

Brett Favre engineers a similar offense to that of the 49ers. He runs the West Coast style offense with great success (winning Super Bow XXXI), but he also has the ability to scramble when things break down.

RISING STAR
Check out Joe's gradual improvement at Notre Dame: 42% completion rate with 12% of his passes picked off as a sophomore. His junior year he completed 52% and had 4% picked. By his senior year he was completing 54% and only 3% were getting intercepted. The change wasn't all that dramatic from year to year, and there was still room for improvement even as a fifth year senior. The point is, little by little, he was heading in the right direction.

you realize that no defense can consistently cover three or four receivers on every play, you'll recognize that your offense has the edge.

You will be hit with a ton of information at the start, but don't let it intimidate you. Find the time to concentrate on it—*at least* an hour a day. The biggest obstacle to absorbing all this information is that a playbook is written in another language. Some—like the one we used in high school—use numerals. At Notre Dame, the plays were 99% words with numerical variations for each formation. Add that type of information overload to the normal pressure of playing quarterback for Notre Dame and leaving home for the first time while pulling down a full courseload and holding down a part-time job—well, once I survived that, I figured I should be able to handle just about anything the future would throw at me.

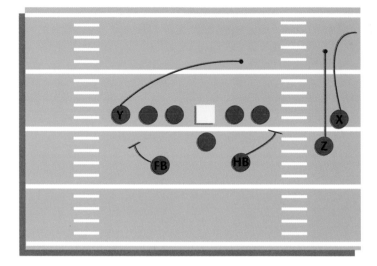

Here is the play diagram for Red Left Slot Waggle Right X Out. Each offensive player on the field will either have a route to run or a specific blocking assignment (in some cases both). The quarterback, however, has to know every player's responsibility.

Bill Walsh's system in San Francisco wasn't any easier to learn. He made my transition to the pros a lot easier than the one I had from high school to Notre Dame, primarily because he worked me into games gradually. Maybe that's a benefit to being a third-round pick—less pressure to put me straight into the starting line-up, more time to figure out what Red Left Slot Waggle Right X Out meant. Besides, we already had a quality young quarterback, in Steve DeBerg, who would go on to have a 17-year career in the NFL.

Believe it or not, my foreign language classes in high school helped me a lot with playbook-speak. With a foreign language, I always repeated the sentence in my mind, first in English, then in German or Spanish (and, these days, Italian). With a playbook, the process is very similar. You see the play, visualize what it is, then match that up with the terminology. It will help that your coaches will be speaking this language to you all season, with no one there to translate for you. It *won't* help that you will constantly be getting new plays during meetings, without having any extra time to study them. If football teaches you anything, it teaches you how to adapt and adjust.

Remember, this isn't memorization. This is *learning*. When you memorize something, you don't adjust to subtle changes very quickly. When you *learn* it—when you know how and why something is being done, and not just *what*—you can react quickly to different fronts and coverages. You need to get to the point where something immediately registers in your mind once the play is called.

Learning the Plays

A game plan can't be mastered without studying the playbook. And I mean *study*. So once I had the offensive philosophy and the terminology down, here's what I would do to learn all those plays: I would physically trace over them in my playbook with a red pen. It helped me to visualize what would be happening on the field. When a play was called, the picture would immediately come into my mind. I would trace the plays at least once a night after learn-ing them, and some-times four or five times during the week.

Then I would go through each play in my head and try to visualize where the players were supposed to be. Then I would visualize the pass patterns—the end of the route, to be exact. I would see the linemen in front of me, then I would concentrate on where the receivers were instructed to end up. You need to visualize what will be happening once the ball is snapped.

Visualization is key even if you're not the quarterback—and is yet another reason Bill Walsh gave all the players the first 25 plays the night before the game. It gave the guys something to look forward to if they knew they were going to get the ball on a particular play. He deviated from the script if we got backed up against our own end zone or took the ball in close, but most of the time the offensive unit went down the field knowing what was going to come next.

The Game Plan

Whether it's Pee Wee, Pop Warner, high school, college, or the NFL, to understand what's in the playbook, you need to understand the team's overall offensive philosophy. What are you trying to do with the ball? When you keep that in mind, the plays in the playbook will begin to fit together and form a picture in your mind—and you'll understand what's expected of you.

"Joe Montana was very analytical. He didn't try to force the ball into situations where it could get picked off. He took what the defense gave him."

—*Johnny Unitas*

A quarterback who can run adds another dimension to an offense, but he has to make his decisions intelligently. There are times when he should wait a little longer in the pocket for something to develop, times he should throw the ball away, and there are times to take off and carry the ball upfield for a gain.

A quarterback's responsibilities will differ greatly, depending on the type of offense that is being run. In Bill Walsh's offense, a quarterback needs to be mobile, capable of handling a complex system, and willing to take what the defense gives. A strong arm isn't so critical—unlike the Oakland Raiders and their "vertical" offense that tries to stretch the defense with deep passes.

When Bill Parcells was coaching the Giants and relying on a smash-mouth running offense, the first priority of the quarterback was to not make any mistakes. Phil Simms didn't need to throw for 300 yards to win, so long as he took care of the football. The same would be true of a lot of high school and college programs—the best example of which might be the old USC teams of the late '60s and 1970s that featured a dominant tailback and lived on power running plays such as "Student Body Right."

Finally, several high school and college teams need a quarterback who can run first and throw second. With little threat of a pass, these teams rely on a size and speed advantage to move the ball on the ground. The quarterback who directs such an offense will have to be fearless, occasionally holding the ball on an option play until the last possible second, drawing defenders to him to free up room for his running back. He may get leveled then, and he'll certainly get nailed a few times when he keeps the ball himself. Often these quarterbacks don't get the credit they deserve, because they don't throw the ball.

In fact, the hardest hit I ever took in my life wasn't delivered by Jim Burt, Leonard Marshall, or Bruce Smith to knock me out of a playoff game. It was one time running the option in practice at Notre Dame, when I got nailed by a guy who later worked in Hollywood. In the movie *The Rock*, he was the marine who got crushed by an enormous block of metal that fell from the ceiling. When I saw him recently, I told him it was about time he found out how that felt.

It takes awhile to get fully comfortable in an offensive system. To be honest, in 1985 I still wasn't fully settled. I wasn't comfortable throwing deep yet, and up to that point, in Bill Walsh's system, we only went deep about one or two times a game—compared to John Elway and Dan Marino throwing long about a dozen times. That changed when we got Jerry Rice and started to stretch the defenses. By the end of 1988 and through 1989 and 1990, we were firing on all cylinders, going 39-6 with Jerry's speed keeping the defenses from collapsing on us.

Obviously, the higher the level, the longer it takes to master the game plan. With Bill Walsh's "West Coast Offense," we wanted to apply constant pressure on the defense. The more pressure we applied, the more success we had. That's why so many teams are trying to run this offense today—such as the Super Bowl champion Green Bay Packers. We didn't go after particular players as much as we went after parts of the field: the left and right "flats" 10 to 15 yards off the line of scrimmage; medium right and medium left, about 10 to 20 yards deeper; and the area underneath the linebackers which always seems to attract a lot of attention. The defense usually tries to control underneath simply by blasting anybody who comes by. That's what the Giants did to Andre Reed in Super Bowl XXV, their big hits essentially taking the Buffalo Bills' best receiver right out of the game after the 1st quarter.

Bill wanted us to attack the defense at its weak spots and make the other team try to stop us. We just went after a vulnerable area. We'd "flood" a zone, putting so many receivers and so many options in a certain area of the field that the defense couldn't possibly defend them all. His attitude was: Here's your weakness, what are you going to do about it?—which is basically the flip side of Vince Lombardi's Packers of the '60s. The Packers would run the power sweep to perfection, saying: Here's our strength, try to stop it.

We executed, we put pressure on the defense like all successful offensive units, but still we were known for finesse and for "nickel-and-diming" people to death with our short passes. Well, I bet you didn't know that the 1984 and 1988 championship teams had a higher-ranked rushing offense than passing offense. As for "nickel-and-diming," no defense wants to be out on the field for a long time, getting beaten down throughout a game. It can be downright humiliating. I know, because I've seen it in their eyes.

We didn't just put pressure on defenses by attacking their vulnerable areas. The sheer complexity of our system made us

"[My rookie season] was a big learning year for me. I knew I wasn't ready then, but I got a chance to start in the pre-season this year, and I'm more comfortable running the offense. I'm not nearly as nervous as I was last year."

—Joe Montana, 1980

"Joe understands the total concept of our intricate system incredibly well for a young quarterback. He makes quick, intelligent decisions during a play when he has to pick and choose his receivers. He knows precisely what is right or wrong with a play as soon as it happens."

—Sam Wyche,
49ers quarterbacks coach,
1981

Walsh and Montana sit at a farewell rally for Joe in San Francisco. Walsh often scripted out the first 25 plays of the game for his offense. Not only did this allow his players to better mentally prepare, it also instilled an attitude in his offense that they would dictate play.

> "Any quarterback can run this system. It's made for a quarterback. Anybody would be successful with it. I happen to fit into it well. On pass plays somebody's always open. I just have to find him."
>
> —Joe Montana, 1985

> "The football field is 53⅓ yards wide, but there are a lot of quarterbacks playing the game—even in the NFL—who don't know that. You've got to play on the entire field, not just two-thirds of it."
>
> —Daryle Lamonica

a very difficult team to prepare for. After talking to players on other teams in the NFL, I learned that most of them have the same 20 or 25 plays each week. But with the 49ers, we always had new plays as well as dozens of old plays. In many games we'd be ready to use around 60 different plays. One game, I remember, we had more than 100 plays—and that's not counting all our different formations.

Our playbook was huge. Most teams only had 15 running plays and 30 passing plays from which to select their weekly game plan. We had 30 running plays and 90 passing plays. We also had two or three formations for most of the passing plays, with the receiver progression changing depending on the defensive alignment. You should have been there when Bill was working the Pro Bowl, which is played mostly for fun: he put in 50 passing plays. The guys from the other teams were whining after the first 30. On the 49ers, we could have groaned and convinced ourselves there was no way we could learn all these—and we would have never accomplished anything as a team. We looked at it the other way—once we get these down, how in the world can any defense expect to know what's coming?

If that wasn't enough to throw at the opposition, Bill Walsh scripted the first 25 plays. Part of the reason for this was that some plays work better when part of a progression. You cross up the defense by running out of a particular formation after you've passed out of it the last three times, for example. The main reason Bill did it, though, was to ensure that we didn't settle into any patterns. Most teams, in preparing for their upcoming opponent, will review the films of that team's previous three games. One of the things they do is chart plays and formations by down and distance. One time, the Giants were looking for tendencies on us and just gave up. Out of 100 first down plays on these films, we ran 100 different plays. So much for tipping off any of our preferences.

The Film Room

Visualization is helped greatly by watching game films. Not everyone will have access to these to prepare for opponents. If you do, take *full* advantage of it. There are ways to get a lot out of game films in a reasonable amount of time, provided you know what to look for.

First, always remember why you're watching the films: to see how you can take advantage of what you and your teammates do well. Remember when I said that the whole thrust of the West Coast Offense was to find a defense's vulnerable areas and go after them? Well, that's what I did when I watched film. I looked for those areas and thought about how I could put my teammates in position to exploit them.

If you're at a level where film of your opponents isn't available, try getting hold of a video camera recording of the game. If your parents are making one for you, they should try it from the sideline as well as a wide angle shot from the corner of the end zone. The end zone shot should give you much better depth perception and reveal things a sideline shot won't. Some of the key things for a quarterback to watch for are whether a defender is a foot inside, half a step one way, or a shade to the outside. These things can tell you whether someone is playing zone or man-to-man. Remember when I talked about a cornerback tipping off man coverage by lining

"Luck is what happens when preparation meets opportunity."

—*Darrell Royal, former head football coach at the University of Texas*

"Most coaches study film when they lose. I study when we win—to see if I can figure out what I did right."

—*Paul "Bear" Bryant*

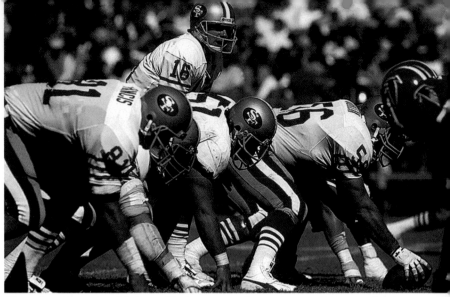

Film taken from the sideline will alert you to formations and the depth of a defensive player's position. A view from the end zone will allow you to see players shading to the inside or outside, which may tip you off to various coverages.

up a shade to the inside? You can't always see that half-step inside from a sideline shot. Whether someone is 10 or 12 yards deep—which a sideline shot will tell you—isn't as important as their inside or outside position.

They call the end zone tickets the "cheap seats," but that's where I'd rather watch a game. I tried for years to get the 49ers' video crew to use a wide angle shot from there, but I was never successful. Mike Ditka's Bears used this shot, but I only learned that recently. NFL teams exchange videotapes before games, but it turns out that Ditka never shared the end zone view with us because we didn't have any of our own to provide.

When you do get your hands on a tape or film, watch it several times, concentrating on a different part of the offense and defense each time. You might watch the safeties one time, the linebackers another. It will be difficult to pick up little details if you're trying to watch all 22 players at once.

Young quarterbacks should take notes. Look at the big plays—a sack or a long gain—and try to figure out why they happened. Identify the weak links on the defense, and note how the offense tried to exploit them. Watch for tendencies that may be tipping off blitzes or coverages. Focus on individual weaknesses rather than players who just might have been out of position. You should assume that any problems with the defensive alignment will be addressed by the opposition's coaching staff. Individual weaknesses take a lot longer to fix.

You need to understand the defense you'll be playing against. You can't understand your offense without knowing how it works against the defense you'll be facing—the guys on the other side of ball—how are they going to line up? What are they going to do if you line up a certain way? What are you going to do if they line up a certain way? This was especially tough with Buddy Ryan's defenses, since he had about as many variables on defense as Bill Walsh had on offense.

When you watch your own team's tapes, check to see if you're doing anything that might give your plays away to the defense. That's the one thing you can count on in football. The other team will be studying you, too. Depending on the level at which you're playing, here are some of the things the other team's scouts will be checking out about you and your offense:

As you break the huddle . . . your basic offensive set and formations;

At the line of scrimmage . . . any snap count tendencies you might have, how often you call audibles and what plays you go to when you do;

As you drop back from center . . . how quickly you get set up in the pocket, whether you telegraph plays by where you look, and whether anyone on your offensive squad is tipping off draw plays, screen passes, or play-action fakes;

As you stand in the pocket . . . who the weakest pass blocker might be, how effectively your running backs can pass protect, how well you can scramble, your "money" receiver and the routes he likes to run.

Try to watch your own tapes not just to identify things you can correct, but from the perspective of a defensive coordinator. What would *you* do to stop your offense? When you're watching defense tapes, keep these things in mind:

At the line . . . their basic defensive set, how often they show blitz, and where their corners and safeties tend to line up;

On rushing plays . . . the role the defensive backs play in run defense, the lateral pursuit the linebackers get on sweeps, and the inside containment the defensive line manages on runs up the middle. How well does the unit handle draws?

On passing plays . . . a "designated blitzer," how often they play zone or a tight or loose man-to-man, whether the linebackers are more likely to blitz or drop back into coverage, how often the pass rushers stunt, and whether the ends try to overpower the tackles on bull-rushes or beat them wide on speed rushes. How well does the unit handle screens, play-action fakes, roll-outs, sprint-outs, and ad-lib scrambles?

Overall . . . any areas or players especially vulnerable to the run or pass, a heavy-pressure or bend-don't-break approach, and any blitz tendencies (down, distance, field position, formation, personnel).

When you can see the offense from the perspective of all 11 positions, and when you know what the defense tries to do to shut things down, the "big picture" should begin to form. It will help if you have developed good working relationships with your teammates and coaches, especially with the head coach and/or offensive coordinator. Ask questions. The quarterback has more interaction with the head coach and offensive coordinator than any other player. What happens when the offense comes off the field? The quarterback usually goes straight to the coach to talk about what is happening, or he puts on the headset and talks with someone in the booth.

These relationships will help you during those times when you have to act like a coach on the field. Learning your offense means learning the routes for the receivers, tight ends, and running backs, and learning the line's blocking schemes—and what will work against any type of defense.

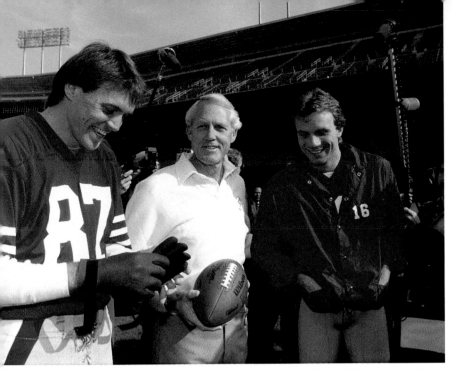

Dwight Clark, Bill Walsh, and Joe Montana at Candlestick Park preparing for their upcoming Super Bowl match with the Miami Dolphins. Joe was able to develop good working relationships with both his coaches and his teammates—something that cannot be taken for granted.

The quickest way to lose your teammates' respect is by being perceived as lazy. No quarterback can win a game all by himself, but plenty have lost games single-handedly by not putting in the effort to prepare themselves adequately. Don't expect it to be very easy to face your teammates in the huddle if you cost them a game because you weren't willing to work hard enough to learn the game plan.

If you're wondering where you're going to find the time to do all this—well, back in high school I don't recall going to very many parties, if any. I had no time. It helped that we didn't have a beach to go to in Monongohela, Pennsylvania— just a river that you couldn't swim in because it was deemed a fire hazard. It probably helped that I wasn't very good at even trying to party. I remember one time someone had gotten a couple of old bottles of wine. I set them outside, by the steps, so my parents wouldn't see them. What happens? My Dad went outside to look for something and, sure enough, that put an end to all of that.

> "People striving, being knocked down and coming back . . . that's what builds character. . . . I've seen very little character in players who never had to face adversity."
>
> —Tom Landry,
> former Dallas Cowboys coach

Perhaps no one has been rewarded as much for sheer perseverance as handsomely as quarterback Doug Williams. Williams struggled mightily in the few playoff games he played in with Tampa Bay (27 of 85 passing, two touchdowns, and nine interceptions) and then departed for the USFL for two years. When the rival league folded, he could have just gone home, but he returned to the NFL as a backup with the Redskins instead. A year later, at 32, he took the starting job from Jay Schroeder and ended up in the Super Bowl against the Denver Broncos. It looked like he'd be out of the game in the first quarter after a shot to the leg, but in the second quarter, he ended up having the greatest 15 minutes any quarterback has had in Super Bowl history, or probably ever will—228 yards passing and four touchdowns. At that time, the four touchdown passes in the second quarter tied a Super Bowl record of four in a game!

ADVERSITY

Let's debunk some myths about successful athletes having an easy time of it. You probably already know about Michael Jordan being cut from his high school basketball team. Larry Bird didn't like it at Indiana University with Bobby Knight and went back home for a year. Willie Mays went 0-for-24 at the start of his big league career. Mario Lemieux came back from both a serious back injury and cancer. We've already talked about the injuries that Phil Simms faced at the start of his career, and the difficulties Terry Bradshaw, Troy Aikman, John Elway, and Dan Fouts had as rookies. Despite appearances, being successful in professional team sports does not come easy for anyone.

There's one thing I can guarantee any young quarterback: you will face adversity. For every "magic moment" I've had, I've been picked off, benched, thrown down, or knocked cold. Every athlete has doubts and low points. Looking back on it, I guess I have my parents and my coaches to thank for my never quitting and never whining when things got rough.

Myth: You're Always "The Man"

My first season on Notre Dame's varsity in 1975, I started out tenth on the quarterback depth chart. I made it all the way to second-string during pre-season, and I got to start against Michigan State when our first-string quarterback, Rick Slager, went down with an injury. We lost 10-3, and I didn't have a very good game at all. Later, I got to see some action in relief and did a bit better. After I came off the bench to help the Irish to two come-from-behind victories, I got the start against USC and didn't do much better than I did against Michigan State. I was getting the reputation as a guy who could help you out off the bench in a desperate spot, but who couldn't get it done as a starter. I didn't like that, but what could I say? You can only change your reputation on the field.

Myth: You Never Lack Confidence

I had to deal with the controversy created by my erratic play. Some people thought I should be the starter, while others pointed out how I only seemed to play well coming off the bench. The other quarterback, Rick Slager, was my buddy, so

Most fans can only imagine Joe Montana as a superstar. But at the collegiate ranks, he had to fight for his playing time just like anyone else.

at least I had someone to talk about all the pressure that this was putting on the two of us. It's hard to play when you're worried about your next mistake meaning a spot on the bench. Football is hard enough without having to look over your shoulder, and you can't play quarterback without confidence.

Myth: A Starring Role is Yours for the Taking

Slager kept the job in '75, but after he graduated, I came in the next season anxious to claim the starting assignment for myself. Then in a pre-season workout, I stumbled coming away from center. Our defensive end nailed me, and I came down hard on my right shoulder. I'd never been seriously hurt in a ball game before, but I knew immediately that this was bad. I ended up sitting out the entire season with a separated shoulder. When I came back in 1977, I was down from second-string to third-string. I had to ride the bench in a road game against Pitt near my home town, knowing that my family and friends who came out to see me play were going to see me carry a clipboard instead. As I said at the time, you have to understand that a coach can play only 11 men and he's going to pick the ones he thinks are his best chance to win. That doesn't help much, though, especially when you're used to starting. As good as our starter was, I've always said that you wouldn't be much of a player if you didn't think you were better.

Myth: The Pressure Never Gets to You

Two weeks after the Pitt game, we were 1-1, coming off a bad loss, and struggling against a Purdue team we should have been beating. Our starter had been pulled, and our backup had his collarbone broken, but I *still* wasn't in the game. (This was the game when I found out I'd dropped from second-string to third-string—a hard way to learn that kind of thing.) I didn't think I'd ever get a chance to play. If I started jumping up and down and screaming about it, I probably never would have. I kept my mouth shut, and with 16 minutes to go, I came in for our starter with Notre Dame down 24-14. I was scared. And I had every right to be. I hadn't thrown a pass in a game in about two years. I knew enough not to want my teammates to know how nervous I was, so I called for a simple, short pass to our tight end. Right. I threw a duck. It was end over end, underthrown, and should have been picked. We ended up winning that game, but I bet few guys on our ballclub would have expected that after the first pass.

Myth: You Don't Care What the Media Says About You

That win against Purdue settled me down, right? Wrong. Next up was Michigan State. I'd stunk it up against them in my first start in college, and I still had in the back of my mind all that talk about how I couldn't get it done as a starter. You try to keep that stuff out of your head, but that's easier said than done. You just have to remind yourself that you know yourself better than anyone else possibly could. That's what I told myself, anyway, even though I could see myself struggling against Michigan State all over again. Well, we won, and it sent us on our way to a national championship, but I really had to work to block the bad memories and media criticism out of my mind.

In a sport where there are 300-pound giants whose sole purpose is to crush the quarterback, playing the so-called "glamour position" can be a haunting experience. Here, Montana is down for the count on the Meadowlands turf after a terrifying hit by New York Giant Jim Burt.

Myth: Injuries Happen to Other People

I see this bulletproof attitude in a lot of younger athletes. It probably helps them play with a degree of fearlessness. Any of that attitude I might have had disappeared in 1986 when I ruptured a disk in my lower back. After the operation, I basically had to learn to walk again, but I managed to make it back to play the last seven games of the year—just in time for Jim Burt to knock me into next week in a playoff game against the Giants. That's the hit that prompted the 49ers to trade for Steve Young. Looking at the tape of me lying motionless on the Meadowlands turf, I can't blame them.

Myth: It's Always Your Day

That loss to the Giants in 1986 was one of seven post-season losses I contributed to. I was knocked out of that game and two others—January 1991 in the championship game against the Giants with a broken hand, cracked ribs and a concussion; and three years later with the Chiefs in the championship game against the Bills with yet another concussion. No losses are easy to take, but these weren't as bad as our 24-

21 loss to the Redskins in the 1983 NFC Championship Game. We were down 21-0 going into the 4th quarter against the Redskins, but we fought back to tie it, only to lose on a field goal with 40 seconds left after a bad call on Ronnie Lott away from the play. If we'd won that game, we'd have gotten to face the Raiders in the Super Bowl. We carried that loss with us a lot longer than most, using it as motivation in 1984 to get back to where we thought we should have been in 1983. Our motivation worked.

Myth: You Walk Out on Top

The last pass I threw was picked off in the red zone in the 4th quarter of a first-round playoff loss to the Miami Dolphins. As the clock counted down, I knew it was my last game. Heck, I'd already told Bruce Smith, "I'm too old for this," during a 44-10 loss to the Bills during the regular season. An injury recap for my two seasons in Kansas City: sprained wrist, pulled hamstring, two concussions, bruised ribs, bruised hip, sprained foot, sprained knee. There were some good times in Kansas City, but I had to learn the hard way that the quarterback position is a tough place to get old.

As the saying goes, "That which does not kill me, makes me stronger." I believe that, in the long run, I was better off for having to fight for a job at Notre Dame and endure some bitter losses in San Francisco. The point is, you pretty much have to count on taking your lumps now and then. Learn what you can from it and move on.

ENTHUSIASM

If you don't enjoy football, why put yourself through the inevitable adversity? With football, you have to want to be a quarterback. You can't be afraid to fail. You can't worry about being in a position with a lot of pressure and needing to be perfect all the time. You must have a certain strength to be able to rebound from an incompletion or interception, because there will be times when a lineman will miss a block, a receiver will miss a pass or a route, or a back might miss a hole—people watching the game might not realize this. The quarterback is the one who gets the blame, or the credit, for the ultimate execution.

"You have to be willing to compete and love to play quarterback. . . . The ones who seem to come across with a lot of confidence would be the ones I would want as a quarterback. That would be the first trait I would look for. They would need to have the willingness to work hard, to put in lots of extra time."

—*John Barnes, Los Alomitos High School head coach*

Keeping the game enjoyable is actually one of those challenges that becomes stiffer the higher you go, as the fan and media attention increases. A lot of guys in the NFL view the game as just a job, and they're missing out on the fun. I never had that problem. You can find plenty of action photos of me on the field where you'll actually see a grin on my face. I never could get that "death stare" that Michael Jordan and Mark Messier have, but that doesn't mean I was goofing around. There's no reason you can't enjoy something that you take very seriously.

Obviously, losing isn't very much fun, but maintaining enthusiasm can be a huge problem for some of the best teams in the league. Complacency sets in. The hunger can diminish. Did you know that eight Super Bowl champs haven't even made the playoffs the following year? After we won the Super Bowl the first time, we went 3-6 during the strike-shortened 1982 season. That was a weird season, with eight teams making it in each conference—and we could have made it at 4-5 if things had broken right for us in the final week.

We had the same problem at Notre Dame in 1978. At a football power like Notre Dame, where anything less than a national championship is considered an unsuccessful season, you're pretty much playing a single-elimination tournament from day one. We weren't ready for that. We lost our first two games, with our offense turning the ball over 10 times, four times on interceptions. We eventually got it together and finished 9-3, but it taught me early on that repeating as champions—especially in football, which requires so much personal sacrifice—is as tough as it gets.

GETTING STARTED EARLY

As a kid, there was never just one quarterback I tried to pattern myself after. I was heavily influenced by Johnny Unitas, Bart Starr, Len Dawson, Joe Namath, Terry Bradshaw, and winners like that. I never tried to be just like them, though. You have to be who you are. Besides, how could I be Terry Bradshaw, with the arm he had? I had an easier time trying to be Len Dawson, throwing in my back yard to Otis Taylor. You have to recognize and accept your strengths and weaknesses as early as possible. Work on the weaknesses,

Many itemize size, speed, and arm strength as the major factors in being a successful quarterback. But without enthusiasm and a love for the game, a good quarterback will never become a great one.

"The hardest part is trying to get people to forget about last year. The national championship means tremendous personal satisfaction, but that was last year. We've got to get it together again now."

—Joe Montana, 1978

When Joe played, he expected to win—every time. But this desire didn't keep him from having fun playing the game.

then try to play to your capabilities. That's what coaches and athletes mean when they talk about "staying within yourself."

Becoming a football fan is certainly a good way for a young player to develop an enthusiasm for the game. Some advice: don't just be a fan of one team; be a student of the game. Take note of what teams play the game the way it should be played and try to figure out why they're consistently successful. The same goes for players. Don't just focus on one guy you happen to like. Study all the winners and see how they do it.

Now, I'd love to be able to tell you that watching a lot of football on television will not only develop your enthusiasm for the game, but teach you a lot about it, too. The truth is, it won't. There is not much you can learn about how offenses and defense attack each other from watching TV. I get really frustrated watching games on TV, because I can't see the whole field and all 22 players. You're really only seeing half of the game, at most.

To learn about football, my advice is to play the game, not watch it. I've always been what I'd call a "do" person rather than a watcher. You have to be to make it in athletics. We always carried balls around as boys, depending on the seasons. I can't remember not having a ball in my hand or a sport to play. That probably helped shape me as a young quarterback more than anything. In retrospect, we worked like dogs but, to us, it was a blast. We would have played 24 hours a day if we could. I can recall playing the first round of a basketball tournament in Pittsburgh on Friday, traveling to Niagara Falls for a tournament on Saturday (we should have won that one), then returning for the final round in Pittsburgh on Sunday (we did win that one).

In addition to getting off the couch and getting outside, there is no substitute for a good mentor as you're learning to play the game. It might be your father, your mother, your coach, or all of the above. You need someone who'll push you, because you can push yourself only so far. It's like when you're working out. You might be able to do three more reps, but you're more likely to do them if your buddy is there to push you.

Growing up, my father was even more critical of me than I was. He continually emphasized the importance of wanting to be perfect. He wouldn't let me settle for "pretty good." That's why my jaw dropped when I was speaking to him after an NFL game one time early in my career. We'd won, but I hadn't played as well as I would have liked. He said, "You've made it where you want to be. Be a little easier on yourself." I was thinking, "Where did *that* come from?"

My father was always able to inspire me without burning me out. I hope I can do the same with my kids, with whatever they want to do: race cars, play piano, be a veterinarian, whatever it is that makes them happy. There is so much opportunity today, so many choices for young boys and girls. Try as many activities as possible—as long as it's fun. It's a mistake when kids get forced into doing things—such as participating in a team sport—when they don't want to. Not only can this ruin a sport for a young boy or girl, but it also can lead to injury. A kid who is reluctant about playing— what I call playing for the wrong reasons, with their parents forcing them or through peer pressure—doesn't have his or her mind into the sport. Then they get careless, and sometimes hurt.

Making sure that quarterbacking stays fun is the key at the PeeWee, Pop Warner, or high school levels—even college and the pros, to some extent. Anybody can be a quarterback—just as long as there is desire and time commitment. You can't do it because someone else wants you to do it. If it doesn't make you happy, you won't be able to work as hard as you have to.

A simple rule to follow, whatever you do: If you're not having fun, you're not in the right place.

TRAINING TO WIN

Everybody knows football is a physical game. Hitting people and getting hit . . . well, not everyone wants to do it. For a quarterback, the hitting people option doesn't really exist, except after an interception. If you want to last as a quarterback, you have to be in excellent physical shape. You'll need to do some all-over body training to develop strength, flexibility, quickness, stamina, and balance.

Having access to a weight room and exercise equipment will make this easier, but you can build up all of this with just yourself, gravity, a little imagination, and a lot of determination. Work out with one of your teammates. It's safer, and you'll work a little harder if someone is there to push you. Football is a team game, but staying physically fit enough to play it is very much an individual challenge.

You'll need to find the time for all of this, but don't sacrifice throwing time to squeeze in an extra hour in the gym. Conditioning is important, but throwing is critical. Remember: the more you throw, the better you'll get.

> "Football isn't a contact sport, it's a collision sport. Dancing is a contact sport."
>
> —*Vince Lombardi*

STRENGTH

Upper Body

There was a time when weight training was practically forbidden for quarterbacks. The belief was that it would rob you of the flexibility you needed to throw the ball. That attitude has changed completely in recent years. Weight-training is now seen as a matter of self-preservation, given the size and power of the defensive players.

When you get to high school, you'll need to strengthen your upper body so that you can take hits and get back up. Lifting weights at an earlier stage of my career may have prevented some of my more serious injuries down the road. I avoided weights in high school, because I was afraid that too much bulk would affect my basketball and baseball playing.

> On the secret to his team's success: "We're warriors. We're not coming out of games when we're hurt. And in the offseason, we'll train harder than anyone. That's what we do."
>
> —*Roger Craig, 49ers running back*

Building muscle mass is very beneficial to a quarterback. He does, however, need to be careful how he strengthens his upper body. Too much muscle development in the bicep and pectoral region can curtail flexibility and affect the throwing motion.

By focusing on repetitions rather than weight, you can build strength without adding too much muscle mass. That bulk may make you look better on the beach, but it will rob you of the flexibility you need to play quarterback.

There is no magic formula for the right amount of weight to lift. On the various exercises I did, I would shoot for a weight level where three sets of 10-to-12 repetitions would be a strain. Other guys would be doing fewer reps, then continuing to add weight and doing it again. That's not right for a quarterback—not to mention the fact that it's a good way to hurt yourself.

If you have access to a weight room, here are some good upper body exercises to work on. A standard *bench press* is a good way to build up your upper body strength. Don't try to lift as much as you can. Focus on a weight that allows you to lift smoothly and cleanly—then add weight as you get stronger.

There are a few twists you can put on this. You can try a *dumbbell bench press*, lifting two dumbbells, which combined half the weight of your barbell press. It's harder than it sounds. You can also do an *inclined bench press* with the barbell, adjusting the bench to lift from an angle rather than completely horizontal. Finally, you can adjust your grip slightly on the bar.

Some weight rooms have equipment to strengthen your neck muscles. Usually it's the offensive and defensive linemen you see working out with these—at least the ones who end up with necks wider than their heads. It's a good idea for a quarterback to build up his neck strength, too. When you get nailed and hit the ground, your head can "whiplash" off the turf. The stronger your neck muscles, the less whiplash you'll get.

You only need to work with weights about two or three times a week, every other day. Toward the end of my career, I only lifted twice a week—Mondays and Wednesdays. I never worked with weights too close to the upcoming games, but I found that working out the day *after* a game helped the blood get flowing and seemed to speed the healing process.

Consult with your team's trainer first, and always work with a spotter.

If you don't have access to weights, just do as many pull-ups or push-ups as you can—then do ten more tomorrow. You can make push-ups more challenging by doing them on your finger-tips, or one-handed, or with your hands further apart—or even while doing a handstand, like Nicolas Cage at the beginning of *Con-Air*!

The stronger you are, the better your chances of surviving the collisions you'll be in. The guys trying to bury you certainly spend plenty of time working out. Think about that the next time you're tempted to skip a few reps.

Arms, Hands, and Fingers

The bench presses I've described will strengthen your shoulders, but they won't do much for your throwing arm. There is no piece of exercise equipment or machine that I've come across that will help you all that much with your throwing. Working out on a rowing machine will help strengthen the muscles around your shoulder joint, and hopefully keep any rotator cuff problems at bay. You can also go through your throwing motion with a five-pound weight in your hand. Stay away from doing dumbbell curls with heavy weights—you want your biceps strong and flexible, not large and tight. The fact is, the best thing for your throwing arm is throwing.

Your throwing will also be helped by hand and finger strength. That will help you grip the ball better. Here are some things you can do to build up your strength which don't involve any fancy exercise equipment:

- laying old sheets of newsprint out on the floor, grabbing them in the middle and crumpling them into a ball—the more pages you use at once, the tougher it becomes;

- squeezing a tennis ball;

- doing wrist rolls holding a 12-inch piece of wood or pipe with a ten-pound free weight attached with a three-foot piece of rope;

- banging out some of your school assignments on a manual typewriter—if you can find one!

If you don't think hand strength is important, go back to a play in Super Bowl XXV when Giants quarterback Jeff Hostetler was sacked for a safety by Buffalo Bills defensive end Bruce Smith. Hostetler was carrying the ball in one hand, trying to elude the rush, and Smith gave him a shot across his right forearm, but he still didn't cough up the ball. The Giants won that game by one point, so you know how critical that play was.

Legs

There are a number of exercises you can do in the weight room to build up your legs—such as half-knee bends and heel raises with the barbell resting on the back of your shoulders, but I felt more comfortable with activities that strengthened my lower body while also building up my stamina. That meant sprinting, bicycling, and other exercises that we'll discuss later.

FLEXIBILITY

All-over body flexibility is vital for a quarterback, not just throwing arm flexibility. It's important to stretch slowly, without any sudden movements. As you become more flexible, you should hold your stretches longer. If you're stretching and doing the weight training properly—more reps, less weight—you shouldn't be pulling many muscles during practices and games.

Your coaches will have specific stretches they'll want you to do. Here are some that I've seen used.

Arm and Shoulder

Since elbows, wrists, and hands warmed up faster, I focused more on shoulder rotation stretches. Think about how your shoulder moves as you throw a football; during stretching, you always want to work in the opposite direction of the way you are using the muscles. You can do that up against a wall, or by doing light isometrics with it in different directions, or by working with a piece of surgical tubing hooked in a door. Another good stretching exercise for both shoulders involves clasping your hands behind your back and slowly lifting them as high as you can.

Neck and Back

A stiff neck or back is something you'll never think much about until you have to play a game with one. Here are some stretches you can do to make sure you'll have full range of motion in your neck and back.

To stretch your neck, stand straight with your hands at your sides, then turn your head to the left as far it can go and hold it. Do the same to the right. Keeping your shoulders relaxed, lean your head to the left as far as it can go and hold it. Do the same to the right. Bring your head forward slowly until your chin is resting on your chest and hold it. Lean your head backward as far as it can go and hold it.

To stretch your back, put your left hand on the middle of your upper back. Grab your left elbow with your right hand and slowly pull your upper body to the right. Do the same for the opposite side of your body. For this next exercise, sit on the ground with your right leg straight. Put your left foot on the right side of your right knee. Put your right elbow on the right side of your left knee. Look to the left as far as you can. Again, do the same for the opposite side of your body. For more stretching, sit on the ground with your knees bent and both feet flat. Place your hands on your ankles and lean forward. This is a simple stretch, but you'll really feel it in your lower back.

Legs

Taking care of your legs is every bit as important as taking care of your arm. A pulled muscle can slow down your drops, mess up your entire throwing motion, and rob you of your agility in the pocket. Here are some things you can do to stretch your leg muscles. To stretch your calves, lean forward and place your hands against a wall with your right leg bent. Keep your left leg straight and your left foot flat on the ground. Bend your arms to lean forward even farther and really feel it in your left calf. Do the same for your right calf. To stretch your groin muscles, sit on the ground with the soles of your feet together. Use your hands to bring your heels as close to you as possible. Put your elbows on the inside of each knee and press down. To stretch your thigh muscles, lie on your right side and take your left foot in your left hand. Pull the heel up toward your butt. Do the same for the right thigh.

Because throwing is an unnatural motion, it's especially important for quarterbacks to stretch out their arms before they grip the football. In Figure 1, pull your elbow back by your head until you feel a stretch in the tricep and shoulder. Pull your arm across your chest (Figure 2) to stretch out the bicep and front of the shoulder. Hold your arm out and point your fingers up toward the sky as shown in Figure 3. Pull back on your fingers with the opposite hand and feel the stretch in your wrist and forearm. The back and mid-section are also extremely important in the throwing motion, especially when throwing on the run. A towel can be useful in these exercises as shown in the Figures 4,5, and 6.

A simple stretch is to sit on the ground with your legs out in front of you. Reach for the big toe on your right foot and hold it for ten seconds. Release and go to the left repeating the same exercise. Continue this until you do each leg four times. You should be able to reach a little further each time.

Finally, lie on your back with your legs straight. Grab your left leg behind the knee and bring it toward your chest, while keeping your right leg straight and toes up. Do the same for your right leg.

QUICKNESS

There's a basketball drill that's good for quarterbacks, too: line drills. You sprint from the end line to the foul line, back to the end line, to the halfcourt line, back to the end line, to the other foul line, back to the end line, to the other end line, and back to the end line. As you can see, this involves starting, stopping, and starting again, and it is a lot tougher than it sounds. On a football field, you can do it with the goal line, 5-yard line, 10-yard line, 15-yard line, and 20-yard line. It helps your quickness, in addition to your stamina.

Simply playing basketball is good, too. That's what I did about nine months a year in high school. Like football, it's full of short bursts. You're always stopping and starting, even after running the full length of the court. It's good for change

Jerry Rice is one of the most dedicated players in the NFL when it comes to conditioning. Here he works on his quickness, which may be even more important to a receiver than sheer speed.

of direction and overall quickness. These types of exercises are better for a quarterback than running around a track for 45 minutes.

The only problem with basketball is the injury factor. I spent a lot of time on crutches because of basketball. Those competitive juices get flowing and you're sliding into the crowd. Or someone on the other team is out to prove something to you, and the next thing you know he's cutting underneath you.

STAMINA

In many ways, football is both a sprint *and* a marathon. As I've said, basketball will help you keep your wind after those short bursts of energy. At the same time, you need to be able to endure the grind of playing four quarters.

Some quarterbacks do a lot of jogging to build up their endurance, but it can be boring and just puts even more pounding on your knees and ankles. I found bicycling and swimming to be better ways for me to get a tough, low-impact workout. It's not so much *what* you do to build up your endurance—such as a lineman I read about who used to drag a pickup truck one mile every day during the summer, something I do *not* recommend—but that you find an activity you're comfortable with and keep at it.

Having someone to work with can be just as important for endurance training as it is for weight training. You'll be helping each other set a brisk pace and not quit.

BALANCE

Balance isn't just for gymnasts. I didn't work on balance much after my first few years in the NFL, but they had me working on it again in Kansas City. Our offensive coordinator, Paul Hackett, had us stepping on boxes, stepping over bags, jumping rope. We would step on these boxes, starting with the left foot then the right foot, as fast as we could for as long as possible. We had to step over bags, back and forth. Paul felt that everything the quarterbacks do when they come away from the center involves leaning and pushing off and rolling up over the big toe as you either reverse-pivot to handoff in the running game, or as you set up to drop back and pass. These footwork drills had us doing all of that.

As for jumping rope—something Dan Marino has done a lot of—that gets a quarterback used to being on the balls of his feet, as opposed to being flat-footed. You can't throw a ball while jumping rope, but if you can get your hands—or, more to the point, your feet—on a mini-trampoline, you might try that. Work with two other people—one to catch the ball, the other to feed you the ball and to tell you when to throw. Throwing while jumping on the trampoline will help you get better at throwing off-balance.

Late in my career, Ronnie Lott introduced me to Tae Kwon Do to help with my conditioning. It not only helped with agility and balance—having a pole jabbed at me to make me move left, right, or duck, as if I was eluding a defender—but it also reinforced the mental discipline necessary to be successful as a quarterback. A serious weight lifting program should wait until high school, but martial arts can be started at a very early age.

Balance and agility can help a quarterback avoid some nasty hits from the defense. Montana is shown here in Kansas City working his way around a Buffalo Bills defender.

NUTRITION

I tried to eat well—low-fat, high-carbohydrate stuff like pasta, chicken, salads, and greens—but junk food would slip into my diet, too. So would red meat. Don't worry about having the perfect diet—just don't eat bacon and eggs for breakfast, then a burger for lunch, and a steak for dinner. I never ate a lot for breakfast—maybe cereal or toast. For lunch, it would usually just be a sandwich. On game days, I never ate much at all until after the game. I would have a snack the night before a game at about 10 P.M., then I'd just have coffee and cereal or a banana for breakfast, and a candy bar before the game. I'd rather play on a semi-empty stomach. This type of eating suited me for an intense weekend—what with the practices lightening up and the mental preparation intensifying.

As soon as a game was over, Jimmy Warren, who oversaw my well-being while I was with the 49ers and Chiefs, would have burgers for us to eat before we got out of the locker room—sometimes even before we were out of uniform. After Super Bowl XXIV, everything got so crazy with the celebration and award ceremony and media interviews, my father and I hid in the coaches' dressing room eating cheeseburgers with Ronnie Lott—while we were still wearing our game pants and undershirts.

PRIORITIES

It wasn't until I was rehabbing from back surgery in 1986 that I began to start taking care of my body as well as I should have. Once you realize you need to do more things to extend your career, you look for any advantage. You realize you've got to do more exercising than you normally would, to stay even with everybody.

We've covered the basics of good conditioning. Do what you like, but don't do it halfway. Get in shape. There's nothing worse than having to run the ball, only to return to the huddle and be too out of breath to talk. The clock will be ticking. If your legs and wind are gone by the 4th quarter, you're gone, too.

Vision

A great athlete's vision may be the physical aspect that is most often over-looked. Ted Williams had great mechanics and was one of the first students of hitting, but it certainly didn't hurt his performance any to have 20/10 vision. Baseball players and golfers are much more likely to be cross-dominant—to be right-handed and left-eyed, and vice versa. This allows hitters to see the ball, and golfers to see the hole on putts, with a dominant eye that is closer to the target. Wayne Gretzky and Pele both have extraordinary peripheral vision, allowing them to make passes as if they have "eyes in the backs of their heads."

Vision is also frequently overlooked in athletic conditioning for quarter-backs, because many don't realize that there are things you can do to improve how well you see. The fact is, the only other athletic endeavors that put as many different demands on the eye as playing quarterback are driving a race car and skiing down a mountain. Quarterback Bob Schloredt led the Wash-ington Huskies to the Rose Bowl in 1960 and 1961—his team won both games, and he was named the player of the game in both—despite being virtually blind in one eye. He is the exception—albeit an extraordinary one. Playing quarterback is hard enough with perfect vision, so here are some ways to get your eyes "in shape."

Visualization

One of the first physical activities that stress affects is vision. You need to fight stress in order to succeed, and you do this through mental preparation rather than physical preparation. If you're in a slump, focus on your mental approach before you mess around with what you're doing physically. Visualizing specifi-cally and realistically what you will be doing will help you move from stressed-out to confident and relaxed. Most people do this with their eyes closed at first, but you will eventually want to be able to do this with your eyes open. *This isn't fantasizing, it's rehearsing.* As they say in one of Joe Montana's favorite movies, *Caddyshack*, "See your future, be your future."

There are many ways to help you improve your ability to visualize specifi-cally and realistically. One is simply a matter of watching enough tapes of the opponents you will be facing that you become familiar with how they line up and how they react to various plays. Another way is to study tapes shot from the end zone behind the quarterback, frame by frame, testing yourself one or two seconds into pass plays as to which receivers will be open. If these tapes aren't available, have your coach draw you diagrams, and concentrate on those. In actuality, you can work on your visualization skills with no props at all, for it is your concentration skills at work more than your eyes.

Visual Reaction Time

Barry Bonds performs a hitting drill where he is pitched tennis balls with numbers printed on them. Not only must he identify the number, he can only swing at the odd-numbered ones. For mere mortals, there are drills you can do that are less difficult but will still help you in reading defenses quickly. One requires only a pad of paper and a piece of cardboard. Have someone draw a large, partially-filled tic-tac-toe grid and then cover it with the cardboard. They'll remove the cardboard for a half-second, then you'll draw what you saw. You can also do this with strings of numbers and letters. As you get better, make the strings more complex and look at them for shorter amounts of time. Do this enough times, and the speed with which you process information visually will increase significantly. Do this while jumping rope, and your ability to focus on a moving object will improve. Do it with headphones on or the TV turned up loud, and your concentration skills will improve, too.

Peripheral Vision

A quarterback's ability to sense the rush and see the entire field is, in large part, a function of his peripheral vision. There are ways to work on this while also working on your balance and your throwing.

The balance drill involves taping four homemade eye charts—four-by-six rows of capital letters on a piece of paper—on a wall, at eye level, about 18 inches apart. Then lay out a 12-foot piece of rope in a snaking pattern about four feet from the wall. Keeping your head parallel to the wall, walk the rope while reading the four letters in the first row of each chart. At the end of the rope, reverse direction and read the four letters in the second row. Continue until all six rows have been read.

The throwing drill involves drawing a three-by-three grid on a large piece of posterboard and hanging it on a wall so that the center square is at eye level. Draw a large, solid circle in the center square and a random number or capital letter in the other eight boxes. Stand about five yards away with a football. (The larger the posterboard, the farther back you can stand, but you don't want to be so far back that it's too easy to read the other letters while focusing on the circle in the middle.) Have a friend call out a letter in the grid. While focusing on the circle, throw the football at that letter. Try this drill while running a sprint-out (see Chapter 6) if you want to improve your ability to focus on a moving object.

These drills only scratch the surface of what a quarterback can do to improve his visual skills. For more information, read *The Athletic Eye* by Dr. Arthur Seiderman and Steven Schneider.

PLAYING THE GAME

I was always motivated more by a fear of losing than by wanting to win. Winning was expected of you. That was the norm—whether it was by 30 points or 3. You were expected to win. If you had a great game, that was no big deal. That's why you were out there. But losing—that was atrocious.

Why did I feel this way? It's probably because of the hard-working area in Western Pennsylvania where I grew up. At a very early age, the importance of winning was drilled into me. I was taught that I should have fun playing the game, but the real reason I was out there was to win. For the people where I grew up, physical sports were a release, and winning was very important to them. You didn't want to let them down.

As for actually going out and winning a football game, there are many phases to it. You may get off to a good start and protect the lead the rest of the way, or you may be knocked off-balance early and then have to make adjustments and mount a comeback. We'll look at each of these, quarter by quarter.

FIRST QUARTER

You will be nervous about how you're going to perform. You should be. You'll have a lot to think about. To maintain your concentration, don't think about anything other than the game plan. There will be a struggle within not to allow other things into your mind. Staying calm, cool, and collected will be essential to maintaining your poise, but it's a skill that will take some time to acquire.

On the field, your first goal is to establish a rhythm to the game—both for your team and for yourself. You want your teammates to be feeling confident, but you also want to get comfortable with your own playing—especially your timing. In the process, you're feeling out the other team, like a boxer,

> "We can take all the trophies and awards we received, add up our victories on a big white sheet of paper, put them into a wheelbarrow, wheel it out to the 50-yard line . . . and tell the team we're playing, 'Look at this.' How much impact do you think that will have?"
>
> —Chuck Knox

> "Every game boils down to doing the things you do best and doing them over and over again."
>
> —Vince Lombardi

Montana is brought down for a sack during the 1st quarter of a game against the Houston Oilers in 1990. It's important not to panic when things go sour early in the game. The quarterback should remain calm and pay attention to why the game plan is not working.

trying to figure out what type of game it will be. Believe me, they're all different.

What you *don't* want to do is set the tone negatively—putting the ball on the ground, forgetting a play, or throwing an interception early. Knowing the plays is something you can control, but turnovers will happen, no matter how well you're playing. The ball might be thrown well, but it gets tipped and then picked off. That's when you really have to be mentally tough—just like getting back up after a big hit. You have to shake the bad luck off and not let *that* set the tone. Your job is to make sure that nothing or no one—the opposition, the fans, the elements, the refs—dictates the tone of the game to your team.

You have to pick up your receiver, if that tipped interception came about because he missed a catchable ball. Sometimes you see quarterbacks chew out their teammates in full view of the fans and the cameras. Now maybe that's their leadership style, or maybe they're just trying to make sure everyone watching knows that the interception wasn't their fault. If that's what they're thinking about during a football game, they shouldn't be out there.

The quarterback's job is to keep things going in the right direction, so the first quarter is not really the time to take chances—unless, of course, you jump out early in the game and want to try to deliver a knockout blow. Even if you fall behind early, you don't want to start taking too many chances. It can be tempting. Maybe you've started out by missing some passes, and you wonder whether your teammates might be thinking that something is wrong. Even if you go a long time without completing a pass, you still have to project a positive attitude in the huddle. That is one of the most difficult aspects of the quarterback's job. As crazy as everything gets, and as you bad as you might happen to be playing, you still have to be the steadying influence.

SECOND QUARTER

The toughest part of the game for the quarterback is not being on the field. The game is not in your control. There's nothing you can do except watch. It's even worse if the other team's offense is out there because of a mistake you made.

It was fairly easy for me to keep the pressure off myself, even in close games, because it was easy to concentrate. It was tough when I was playing poorly and nothing I did seemed to make it any better. That's when you have to focus on your job and let everyone else do theirs. You can't be thinking about their job when you've got your own to worry about. You have to trust that they care enough about what they're doing to be able to stay on top of the game and do their best.

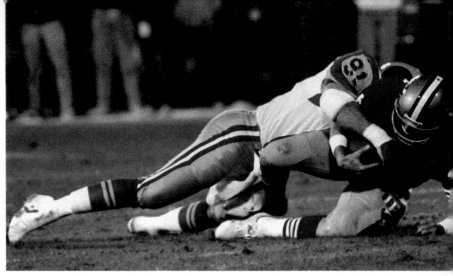

During this 1988 Sunday night game against the Rams, Montana was sacked seven times in the first half. Adjustments are made by the coaching staff at halftime, or right in the booth as the game progresses.

If they don't, or if they haven't prepared, no amount of screaming and yelling in the middle of the field is going to make any difference.

For me, falling behind was always very frustrating. You play the game, you expect to win. You plan something, you expect it to work. Offense is not fun when things aren't working well during a game. You'll know right away when it isn't. There will be times when you say, "Oh, boy . . ." because you're getting the same plays called over and over again and they haven't worked yet. Adjustments are being made right in the booth, because the defense isn't playing you the way you expected. The guys in the huddle are pressuring you to change the plays, but if you change things at their suggestion and it still doesn't work, then you're really in a tough spot. I was confident that if we did what we were supposed to do, we could make the plays work against anyone, so I tried to stick with the game plan for as long as I could.

If nothing seems to work, the coach might have to pull you. He might just be trying to adjust the offensive approach, going with a more mobile quarterback against a heavy pass rush, or going with a stronger-armed quarterback against a defense that's smothering the run and daring you to go deep. He might be trying to shake up the offense. Or maybe you're just not playing particularly well. Whatever the reason, don't whine about it. Everyone wants to play, but being disruptive about having to take a seat isn't going to accelerate your return to the starting lineup. It happens to all of us at some point. I had a lot of trouble as a starter in my early days at Notre Dame, and I got pulled in a playoff game in 1987. Even after I'd made it to the pros and had been a part of two championship teams, there were no guarantees.

HALFTIME

Halftime is usually when a lot of changes are being made by the coaches, all in just 12 minutes, during which you may need to find the time to change gear and make a trip to the bathroom. Formations will be altered based on the outcome of a previous play or series. That doesn't leave much time to even joke around during halftime. The coaches go over exactly how they want to start the second half. You get a drink, and the next thing you know it's time to go back out.

No matter how well the opposing defense might be playing, you can't just throw up your hands and give up. For one thing, a lot of offenses simply stop themselves—through penalties, bad turnovers, delays of game, and an overall failure to execute. (That's not always easy to tell on TV, but it's something to watch for. Is the defense doing this to them, or is the offense doing it to themselves?)

Sometimes a defense can play so well that the offense is shown what needs to be done to beat them. By anticipating so well on plays, a defense can reveal exactly what it will do against a certain offensive set. Then if you line up in the same formations, but run misdirections, play-actions, and reverses instead, you might be able to turn their overpursuit against them.

Take, for example, a game we played in 1989 in Philadelphia against the Eagles. Buddy Ryan's defense had sacked me seven times in the first three quarters. Meanwhile, our running game had been held to eight yards. They had us down 21-10. Finally, we figured out how to pick up their blitzes, which gave me the time to find the open receivers. We scored on four touchdown passes and gained 227 yards through the air in the 4th quarter to pull out a 38-28 win.

Montana celebrates a 68-yard scoring pass to teammate Jerry Rice. The 49ers' incredible comeback over the Eagles at the Vet in 1989 was a prime example that a football game is indeed four (not three) quarters in length.

If that history of football in the Appendix of this book reveals anything, it's that every defense can be exploited . . . eventually.

THIRD QUARTER

Obviously, your attitude when nursing a lead will be different than when you've fallen behind, but not as much as you might think. Some things remain constant: confidence in the game plan, faith in your teammates, and a belief that, if you execute, you can't lose.

If we had a big lead, I might let myself have a little fun. If you were watching me during one of those blowouts when I was on the sidelines talking on the phone, you might have been wondering what intricate facet of offensive strategy I was discussing with my offensive coordinator up in the booth. Well, if it was in one of those stadiums where I could get an outside line, I might have been talking to my wife. If not, I was calling the booth and finding out what kind of food they had up there.

Then there were the nail-biters. Some games are real chess matches, with situations, time, and score dictating every team's move. Think about that Monday Night Football game in 1990 against the Giants, one of the most-watched regular-season games in history. We were both 10-1 and well on our way to an NFC Championship Game showdown. We won 7-3, but that was still a frustrating game in a lot of ways. On offense, even when you're ahead, you can get a little frustrated in low-scoring games like that and do things you wouldn't normally do. Don't. The last thing you want to do when your defense is playing that well is to lose the game 10-7 on an interception return. Let's just say that this particular defensive struggle with the Giants was a fun game—once it was over.

The Giants played us tougher than any other team, because they collapsed their coverages on us and challenged us to beat them deep. Most teams that played us the way the Giants did weren't able to mount much of a pass rush—but most teams didn't have L.T. playing outside linebacker. We lost five playoff games when I was in San Francisco, and three of them were to the Giants. We were held under 20 points

On being pulled after throwing four interceptions: "I thought it was a hell of a move."

—*Doug Williams, quarterback*

Joe may be talking to the offensive coordinator up in the booth about the opposing defense. However, if the game was going well, Montana (shown talking on the phone) may have been checking with security about post-game cheeseburgers.

only three times in post-season, each time by the Giants. They held us to one touchdown in those games—and that one was on a big play by John Taylor when the defender took a chance and went for the interception. So much for sustained drives.

We beat the Giants twice in the playoffs, but even those were tough games. We won 21-10 in 1984, but I threw three interceptions. It was never easy. Against tough defenses like the Giants, the quarterback—especially in our system, but really with any offense—has to be willing to say, "Hey, I don't have to get everything here all at once." It doesn't matter how many plays it takes to score. Still, some people aren't willing to do that. The longer you're out there, though, the fresher your defense will be. Take the short passes if that's what they're giving you. This isn't the prettiest pass for an offense. Fans like to see the ball thrown downfield, but in our case, the pass was part of the running (possession) game.

Montana rifles a touchdown pass against the Giants in a 1984 playoff victory.

The New York Giants defense always put Montana to the test in the post-season. The Giants put an end to San Francisco's season on three occasions during Montana's career. Joe recalls throwing three interceptions during the 49ers 21-10 playoff victory over New York in 1984, but what he fails to add are the three touchdown passes he threw to send the Giants packing.

Don't worry about what the people want to see, and don't try too hard to make the highlight reel. Just win the game.

FOURTH QUARTER

There are a few things a quarterback needs to remember when his team is behind late in the game. One is that you need to try to do *something*, not *everything*. Another is that you shouldn't be asking yourself, "What do I have to do to help us win?" Ask yourself, "Who do I have to get the ball to help us win?" If you want any more evidence that the quarterback is just one of 11 guys, take a look at the only unbeaten team in recent history. The 1972 Dolphins went 17-0, and their starting quarterback, Bob Griese, was out most of the year with a broken leg. They piled up most of their victories with 38-year-old Earl Morrall taking care of those handoffs to Larry Csonka and Jim Kiick.

When you're down, your leadership skills may be more important than your playing ability. The game's not over. I used to tell our guys, "We're not playing well, but from this point on let's be the team we know we can be. If we lose, we at least know we're playing better. Let's stop making stupid mistakes." If you stay positive, things start turning around, and in most cases, you've still got plenty of time. When we were down 35-7 at halftime to the Saints in 1980, we had time to win it 38-35 in overtime, and we did it with four scoring drives of more than 75 yards. You don't get back by throwing deep, or by trying to do it immediately. That might even work against you. The more you control the ball, the more frustrated the defense gets. Meanwhile, their offense is on the sidelines, getting cold.

Then there are the last-minute, down-by-six comebacks. People ask me a lot about those two-minute drills where an offense that's been stuffed all day suddenly starts moving the ball. Sometimes it's a matter of the defense playing a "prevent defense," giving you the short passes to protect against the bomb. Other times it's got nothing to do with the defense and everything to do with the attitude in the offensive huddle. At crunch time, the focus is raised—on good teams, that is. The attitude becomes: "This comeback—it's got to be done. We've been here before, so we're not afraid. It's no big deal."

The quarterback has to perform as an actor inside the huddle at times like this. Nervousness tends to spread in this type of environment. Most players get nervous—even the stars. If that happens, other guys will get nervous because the guy next to him is nervous. That's why you need to act like a comeback is no big deal, even if your stomach is turning cartwheels.

At times like this, quarterbacks, receivers, and backs can't be afraid of getting the ball. At the same time, you can't demand the ball. Let your team play. The get-me-the-ball attitude takes away from your teammates. You just need to be

"I keep thinking Joe Montana's been at Notre Dame for something like eight years. . . . Seems like every year you keep reading about him pulling out ball games."

—Joe Theismann, former Notre Dame quarterback, 1978

"Air Coryell"

The greatest passing dynasty in the history of the NFL is the "Air Coryell" San Diego Chargers of 1979–86. These teams led the NFL in passing six times in eight years, including an unprecedented five years in a row. Of the top ten teams in passing yardage for a season, five are Don Coryell's Chargers teams from the early-'80s.

Dan Fouts, John Jefferson, Wes Chandler, Charlie Joiner, and Kellen Winslow were often victims of their own quick-strike successes. Rarely able to mount long, time-consuming drives to protect an already overmatched defense, the Chargers frequently found themselves in shoot-outs—often on the wrong end. They lost 26 times when scoring more than 20 points, 10 times when scoring 30 points, and even once when scoring 40 points. Compare that to Joe Montana's 49ers from 1983–90.

When scoring	1979–86 Chargers	1983–90 49ers
20-29 points	29-26	43-9
30-39 points	21-10	39-0
40+ points	20-1	14-0

They say that the best defense is a good offense—but only when that offense can take its time scoring.

ready when it comes your way. Just like basketball. If the coach wants you to inbound the ball, inbound the ball. If the coach wants the ball to come to you, be ready for it.

You need to maintain your focus. That's all I think being "in the zone" really is. You're just in a higher state of concentration, where everything seems a lot clearer. It's when you let your mind wander that you make mistakes. You start thinking about bad things that have happened and good things that could happen. Your mind is not where it should be—on this play, right here, right now. Staying "cool" isn't easy—you have to work at it. I got nervous. I got scared, too—like in the 1981 NFC Championship Game against the Cowboys, when I threw my third interception late in the 4th quarter with the Cowboys up 27-21. If you don't get nervous or scared, you're not human. All you can do is try to keep your mind *off* that by keeping it on the game plan.

That's the way it has to be with quarterbacks when you're trying to mount a comeback. Sometimes you'll pace back and forth on the sideline, but that might be the most outward emotion you'll show. In most cases, you're focused on winning the game, so you're thinking about what you've just talked about on the phone with the coaches. You're concentrating on what the coaches had to say, what the plans were, what was going to happen, and what you're going to do about it. If you can do that, you really won't have much time to think about anything else.

THE DRIVE

In Super Bowl XXIII, we had the ball on our own 8-yard line with 3:10 left in the game, and we were down 16-13 to the Bengals. Inside the huddle, we just knew there wasn't anything that was going to stop us from getting a field goal, even though we'd had trouble moving the ball the whole game. We'd been in the situation before. We just knew that if we methodically did our thing, then there should be no reason why anyone would stop us. We'd been doing it all year. We'd always end practice with a two-minute drill, and we'd be going against the best defense we could play—our own. Nobody was better and nobody knew us better, so if we could move the ball against them, we figured we should be able to move it against anyone.

Looking at the list of plays now, it seems shorter than it was. That drive felt like it lasted forever. Initially, all we were thinking at that point was that we had to get into field goal range, so we didn't feel like we were in that much of a rush. We only had to get to the 25-yard line to give us a shot to tie the game. Of course, in the back of my mind, I thought that if we did get down there with enough time, we could start going for the end zone. All we were really trying to do was control the ball and keep getting first downs. That was our whole two-minute offense philosophy: get the ball to somebody who could keep it moving forward.

On first-and-ten, we ran a play to Roger Craig. It was something we had run all the time, where the tight end goes down the middle, then the tailback comes in behind him. If we get a two-deep zone, you throw the ball down the middle to Roger, because most of the time, the linebacker will be

Montana celebrates a touchdown pass during a 38-16 victory over the Dolphins in Super Bowl XIX. Fortunately for Joe and his teammates, no comeback was necessary in this game as San Francisco never trailed Miami after the second quarter.

This diving effort by Jerry Rice tied the score at 13-13 during the third quarter of Super Bowl XXIII. Cincinnati went ahead 16-13 on a field goal, setting up the legendary "drive" engineered by Montana.

picking up the tight end and running with him. If he sticks with Roger, the tight end will be open. If it's not a two-deep zone, Roger reads that and hooks off underneath. We also had Jerry Rice sitting out on a hook if they managed to cover both inside receivers. It's a play mainly devised to get the ball to Roger so that he could turn it up the field for five yards. He got eight.

We went right into another play we ran all the time—a pass to tight end John Frank for seven yards and a first down. We had guys running hooks on the outside. John ran a hook in the middle. He was to find a hole between the two line-backers. Unfortunately, they covered everything—so I threw it low, and he made a good catch down in the dirt for the first down. Then we just threw a quick out to stop the clock. We hit Jerry Rice on the outside, in the right flat, for a seven-yard gain. We had it second-and-three at the 30-yard line.

At that point, we went with a run, with Roger Craig going over the right side for a one-yard gain. We figured we had plenty of time, while they figured we were going to throw. There were two minutes left, and we were still deep in our own territory, at our own 31. But we weren't frustrated. It was third-and-two, and we knew we would go for any fourth down anyway—although the fourth down would have probably been a pass. So we ran Roger a little wider on the second run and he picked up four yards and a first down.

Unfortunately, Roger didn't get out of bounds, so we had to call timeout. We still had two left. During the timeout, we decided to go next with a corner route down the left sideline to Jerry Rice. He pulled it in for 17 yards and a first down, but he also stayed in bounds.

We got right back up, this time on the Bengals' 48-yard line, and ran Roger Craig on the same play that started the drive. This time, he split the middle for 13 yards. He got up underneath, inside the linebackers. He made a good run down the middle, as he always did, busting for an extra two yards or so. First-and-ten at the 35.

This is when I started to hyperventilate. I was so excited about what we were trying to do, and I was trying to scream as loud as I could that it took all the oxygen I had. I started to black out at the line of scrimmage. It was only for a split second, but it felt like it was forever. I could feel my focus start to go away, but, as soon as I snapped the ball and stepped back away from the center, it came back again. Not all the way, though—more like blurry reception on a black-and-white television. Jerry was wide open, but since I couldn't see completely, I ended up just throwing it away, to make sure it went out of bounds. I didn't tell anybody what had happened because I didn't want to come out.

Second-and-ten. The next play was a pass to Roger Craig over the middle—the same type of play as the other passes to Roger—but it was nullified by a ten-yard penalty. One of our linemen was called for being an ineligible receiver downfield. He must have been too anxious to get out and block for him. That penalty put us at the Bengals' 45-yard line, with 1:22 left, second-and-20. Now we really had to start thinking about the field goal, because we had just gotten pushed back, and there was just a little bit of time left.

Then Jerry Rice ran a little hook into a combination of man and zone defense. He caught it on the run and turned it into a 27-yard gain over the middle. He's hard to bring down on the first tackle, anyway, so he got around the first guy and took it to the 18-yard line with about a minute left.

We began to start thinking about the end zone again, not just the game-tying field goal. Still, we ran a possession pass at that point—the same play we had run earlier, with the tight end going down the middle. If something works, stick

"Joe Montana is not human. I don't want to call him a god, but he's definitely somewhere in between. We had them, first down on their 8-yard line, with three minutes to go [in Super Bowl XXIII], and somebody came up to me and said, 'We got 'em now.' I said, 'Have you taken a look at who is quarterbacking the 49ers?' That's what it comes down to. He's maybe the greatest player who ever played the game."

—Cris Collinsworth, former Cincinnati Bengals wide receiver

Montana, Taylor, and Randy Cross (51) celebrate the game-winning touchdown. The 49ers marched 92 yards in under three minutes to claim their third Super Bowl title in the 1980s.

with it. We were actually looking more for the tight end on this one, but he was covered, so we ended up giving the ball to Roger again. He split the linebackers for a gain of eight to the 10-yard line.

With only 39 seconds left, we had to use our second time out. We knew we had time to take two shots at the end zone before we would try a kick. Since they were playing a two-deep zone, we called a pass with an adjustment to the route usually run by John Taylor. Normally on this play, he would be inside and run a hook to the outside, but we called an adjustment to the route—something called "X Up"—which took him straight up the field. Like every football play, even the guys who aren't getting the ball are a critical part of

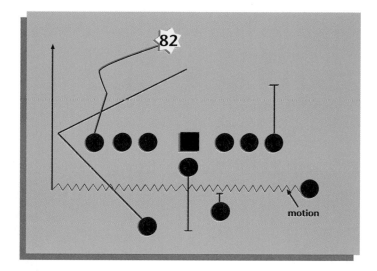

Here is the play diagram for the game-winning touchdown against the Bengals in Super Bowl XXIII. Because the primary receiver (Roger Craig) was lined up wrong in the backfield, Montana quickly decided to look for John Taylor. He found him, throwing what Montana labels as the best pass he ever threw in his career.

making it work. Roger Craig was the primary receiver. Jerry Rice was the decoy, out in the left flat. Meanwhile, John Frank's job was to occupy the safety closest to him—to keep him wide, just enough so that we could squeeze the ball into John Taylor if Roger was covered.

That was the plan, anyway. We got the right coverage, but when I looked back over my shoulder, I saw that the backs had lined up wrong. It could have been a big disaster had the Bengals blitzed us from my right side. They didn't. The backs ended up doing what they were supposed to do, only backwards. So I threw the ball to John Taylor instead of Roger and John caught it for the touchdown and the game. As I said before, it was probably the best pass I've ever thrown.

Actually, this drive is still pretty fresh in my memory, mostly because what we did in the two-minute offense—with the exception of a few plays we'd mix in depending on the opposition—were all plays we had run a million times in practice, every day, every week, usually from day one in training camp. They were all plays that everybody knew. We could have run them in our sleep. That's how Bill Walsh designed it.

> "It's not so much that I relish pressure. I just don't fear it."
>
> —Joe Montana

MONDAY TO SUNDAY

In the NFL, Monday is for healing, Tuesday is for resting, and Wednesday, Thursday, and Friday are for working hard in practice, getting ready to do it all over again on Sunday.

In the pros, we always had Monday mornings off—at least to a certain degree. In San Francisco, we had the entire morning off. In Kansas City, we had to come in and lift by age groups, so Marcus Allen and I were always the last ones. It's nice to know that getting old has some advantages. The young guys had to be in there by 8:30 A.M. Brutal.

GAME WEEK

The day after a game is not a good time to stay inactive. You want to loosen up the arm—unless it's really sore. The true Monday morning quarterback should throw a little, because that's how you can keep your arm strong and be ready to go again on Wednesday. Besides, it's not so much the throwing you do on Sunday that wears you down. It's the beating you take during the game. Hip pointers are bad—there's just nothing you can do about it and it feels like the bone has pinched the muscle. If you get a bruise or a turf burn, though, and you leave it unattended, it will become twice as bad by Wednesday. As far as lingering problems go, artificial turf is the worst. Ask anyone who ever played on the stuff. Coach John McKay called it fuzzy concrete, and he wasn't far off. At night, the burn sticks to the sheets. The turf burns never go away during the season. I had one on my leg from a slide made in Kansas City that still looked nasty entering the *next* season.

On Monday, you want to get the body moving, get the blood flowing, which helps get those bumps and bruises feeling better. You want to use a Jacuzzi or a stationary bicycle, something that doesn't have a lot of impact. I tried to get massage therapy on Monday or Tuesday nights. That

Joe Montana enjoys a day on the golf course with fellow Hall of Fame quarterback Johnny Unitas. Golf was an outlet for Montana to relieve some stress from the daily grind of the football season.

really helped get things moving. It always felt good, so that helped with the recovery during the week, no matter what. I used acupuncture and chiropractic techniques, too, but these should not be used by anyone younger than the collegiate level. There were times when my back pain was so great that nothing helped, so I'd have to get an epidural injection to put the medicine right on the nerve. Then the chiropractor would try to massage it and loosen things up, trying to put things back into place, getting the hips back the way they needed to be so that I wouldn't walk crooked. He'd crack my elbow, my shoulder, my neck, you name it. This should not be done without proper consultation by qualified professionals, especially for quarterbacks who aren't yet fully grown into their bodies.

By the time you get to the second day after a game, the body is ready for a true day off. That means you can relax more and enjoy yourself much more than having the day off immediately following a game. Try to have a normal day. Relax. Play golf. Hang out. For the high school or college-level athlete, take some time and do something other than playing and studying football. Do some school work. Go to a movie. Have some fun. Just give the body a break . . .

. . . because Wednesdays, Thursdays, and sometimes Fridays, are long days. In San Francisco and Kansas City, we might get to work about 7:30 A.M., and we might stay as late as 6 P.M. We'd have meetings most of the morning, an hour for lunch, a long afternoon practice, and then more meetings afterward. You could never get players to fully concentrate at those late meetings. Some would actually fall asleep.

That's what Friday nights were supposed to be for. I rarely slept much the night before a game, so Friday night was the most important night to sleep. As long as I rested that night, I felt pretty good about Saturday night, no matter how much I sat up thinking about the game and the plays. I always studied the night before a game. I'd trace over the plays, so they would be stuck in my head. I always had to go over the formations, too. Fortunately, our game plans didn't vary as much from game to game as you might think. Formations varied more than the plays themselves. We learned that certain formations do certain things to different teams, putting them in man or zone. With all that preparation and, to some extent, apprehension, I'd get four or five hours of sleep, at the most.

You don't want to do things much differently when preparing for a Super Bowl, but the media crush forces your hand. You start practicing two weeks in advance and it feels like just another game, but it's totally different once the team arrives at the Super Bowl city. All of a sudden you feel the excitement of the game. It didn't matter where we were— Detroit, Palo Alto, Miami, or New Orleans—it suddenly became very clear that this was not just another road game.

First, you can't go anywhere. You can try, but it's a mess. Attempting to get away from the pressure is almost impossible. Meanwhile, practices start to get too intense. Guys on your own team start fighting. They're so ready to play, so anxious and nervous, that it only gets worse as game day approaches. The coaches really had to tone things down as the game got closer, because people were hurting each other. We had players fighting in the hallway of the hotel a few nights before Super Bowl XXIV in New Orleans. Jim Burt won by TKO. Throw that in with one bomb threat and innuendo—and it was a great week.

You can't go out in public without being hassled, so you end up ordering a lot of room service and renting a lot of movies—and studying. The only playbook I ever saved is from our second Super Bowl. You can see the red marks all the way through the pages where I drew over the plays, over and over again. By the time I was on the field, everything was processed to the point where the game plan was natural. That's the best way for a quarterback to prepare—to concentrate on the task at hand.

NERVES

A lot of people talked about how cool and mechanical I was, but I was always nervous before the game. Basically, there is a window of time before and at the beginning of the game during which you can be nervous. It's more nervous energy than it is anxiety. You get over it. Failing to acknowledge it, though, can be detrimental. Just expect it will happen and work through it.

"Fear of failure is the worst thing that can happen to an individual. . . . We want to be properly prepared for anything in a game, but we don't want to worry about losing the game. If we lose it, we'll find out why—but one of the reasons shouldn't be that we were so tight we were afraid at the outset. That's terrible."

—*Chuck Noll*

Because I understood and accepted my own nervousness, I was able to know what to look for in my teammates. I liked to see a guy who was nervous, up to a point. If he's nervous about something, that tells me he's concerned about how he performs. Usually the guys who work the hardest and who care the most about what they're doing are nervous, while a lot of other guys are having fun and don't really care how they do. They're just happy to be there. That attitude won't help you win.

It's good to see some nervousness come out in the preparation for a game. Maybe these guys are doing things correctly but are still upset about dropping a pass or forgetting a play. That's the kind of thing I like to see. Not the kind of nervousness where a guy is sitting and staring, too frightened to execute. You want to see the kind of nervousness that makes a player spend more time preparing because he's trying to be perfect.

After a long week of preparation, pregame was a time of eager anticipation. Here Joe loosens up before the game—without having to contend with a wet field or hostile crowd.

The key to controlling your nerves and staying calm—no matter what kind of game—is to develop concentration skills. Golf legend Jack Nicklaus says that when he is standing over a putt, a gun could be fired and he wouldn't hear it. As long as you are concentrating on what you are doing, and thinking about what you've got to do, it's almost impossible for anything else to get into your head. You have to work at that kind of concentration. When former New York Knick and U.S. Senator Bill Bradley was practicing alone as a kid, he would frequently yell, "Concentrate!" at himself if he felt his mind wandering.

There is no substitute for concentration. On the field, you won't be able to simply think about the next play. You'll need to remember the formation, make sure the guys are lined up correctly, and know what to look for in the defense and what to do when faced with different alignments. Things happen so fast on the field that you should already be previewing

"What Bill always drummed into us was winning on the road. He talked about how it was us against the entire city, about how tough we had to be, about what a thrill it would be to take that win away from that team in its home stadium."

—*Randy Cross, former 49ers center*

those events in your mind. That way when a change does happen, you already know how to react. If you have to stop to think about it, it's already too late. This isn't like filming a commercial, where you'll get the chance to redo it if it doesn't work.

ON THE FIELD

After staying in a hotel, there was no more beautiful sight than the stadium. Then, once I was suited up, there was no more beautiful sight than the football field—especially a dry field with no wind.

In addition to bad weather, which we discussed in Chapter 3, another element you may have to cope with is someone else's home field. It was very tough to play in places like Soldier Field, RFK, and the Meadowlands. Bill Walsh used to get us in the right frame of mind. He'd say: "They gotta live here. We just have to be here for three hours and then we can go home."

You can hear the crowd when you're warming up on the football field. If you're on the road, some of the things you hear make you wish you were warming up somewhere else. After a certain amount of time, the stadium noise will fade out. You'll hear certain things when you're not deep in concentration, but in most cases, you won't hear the crowd. People are yelling at you from behind the bench, but half the time, you don't hear them. Then there are places like New York, where players on the sidelines are always making bets as to who will get called the worst name.

You can't let yourself get intimidated—not by a hostile environment, not by the "bullies" of the league. At pretty much any level you play, there'll be that team which has a reputation for playing really tough defense—sometimes beyond tough and into dirty. Like any bully, they won't know how to handle it if you don't blink. Don't let them make you do things you don't ordinarily do. Take *your* game right at them. They won't be used to that, and it could put them back on their heels.

There are some elements I had to contend with that no one should have to endure. Death threats, to be specific. Two of them. One time a police officer told me about it before a

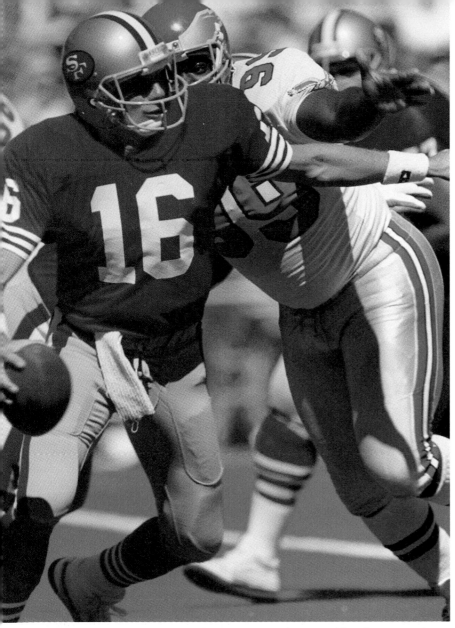

Constant pressure from Buddy Ryan's 46 Defense could make Veteran's Stadium a troublesome playing field for visiting quarterbacks.

game, and nobody would stand by me, or even get near me, on the sideline. I would walk by and people would move. I would go sit on the bench and people would move.

The first threat was prior to a Dallas game in 1982, the year after we beat them twice to go to our first Super Bowl. A

Joe lines up to take the snap during Notre Dame's 1977 battle against USC. The Irish were a tough host that day, pounding the Trojans 49-19.

pair of cops lived with us for two weeks. They even scared one nice old lady. She comes up to me, sets down her shopping bag, and asks for an autograph—and the cops swarm her. The other time, we were at a hotel when they kicked out a girl who was looking for my room. She had three knives. She actually knocked on the door next to mine. At one point I walked past her in the hallway, but she must not have recognized me.

GAME DAY

As the years pass, players realize it doesn't really matter who the opponent is. Anyone can beat anyone at any time. Often a team will relax because you'll be facing a seemingly weaker opponent. Then you get beaten by a team that couldn't carry your equipment, and you find yourself in a race for the division title, a first-round bye, and home-field advantage. It was a race you wouldn't be in if your team hadn't taken it easy at some point during the season. All you had to do was play a normal game. That's why you need to discipline yourself to look no further than your next opponent, even if you will be facing a big rival in two weeks.

Every now and then, you hear about a football coach doing something to really fire up his team for that big rival. Dan Devine did that for us at Notre Dame in 1977, when he brought out the green jerseys for a game against USC in South Bend. They'd been in mothballs since 1963. That sure got the crowd fired up, and it certainly didn't hurt us any. We won 49-19 and were suddenly a contender for the national championship. Most of the time, though, it won't be a big game, and you'll have to be able to motivate yourself.

It's important not to think too much about why you might or might not win the game. Just play. At Notre Dame, we had to face the top-ranked Texas Longhorns in the Cotton Bowl in 1977. We were fourth in the nation, they had Earl Campbell, and it was basically a home game for them. Even if we did pull off an upset, what were the odds that both the #2 and #3 teams would lose? Some teams might have thought about it too much and figured it made sense just to mail it in. We didn't. We concentrated on Texas and let everything else take care of itself. We won 38-10, both the #2 and #3 teams were upset, and we ended up national champions.

In San Francisco, it was a good thing we didn't read the papers or do the math back in 1981. We were 1-2 to start the season, which meant we'd lost 26 of 35 since I'd been there. The odds were 40-1 against us to win division, 60-1 to make the Super Bowl. Fortunately, we didn't pay any attention to that stuff, which is part of the reason we won 15 of 16 the rest of the way.

In big games with the 49ers, Bill Walsh concentrated more on keeping us loose than anything else. When we arrived at the hotel in Detroit before Super Bowl XVI, I remember when I got off the bus, this scraggly old guy tried to grab my bag. I wrestled with him for a moment, then I tried to give him a tip, which he wouldn't take. Finally I figured out it was Bill, dressed as a reporter.

Then, on Sunday, we're on the bus and heading to the Silverdome. Vice-President Bush's motorcade had stopped traffic, so we're sitting there, about to be late to our first Super

On playing at Notre Dame: "Tradition plays a big part here. It comes up a lot, and it's not any cornball stuff. You just don't want to let a lot of people down, because it means so much to so many to uphold the tradition. Everyone is aware of it, and when things begin to go bad a bit, you hear about it a little more."

—Joe Montana

On why the 49ers kept winning: "It's expected of us."

—George Seifert,
former 49ers coach

"We were on the field during our pregame warm-ups for Super Bowl XIX, so I go over to talk to Joe as he is throwing. And he keeps talking about this one part of his delivery that he really needs to work on for next season. And I'm thinking, 'My God, this is the Super Bowl. Why is this guy thinking about next year?' But that's how he was. Attention to every detail. He wasn't joking."

—Paul Hackett,
49ers quarterbacks coach

Walsh, Montana, and owner Eddie DeBartolo, Jr., hold up the Super Bowl trophy after the 49ers defeated the Miami Dolphins 38-16 in Super Bowl XIX.

Bowl. Bill starts talking, telling us not to worry, because he was listening to the game on the radio, and Chico Norton, our equipment manager, had kicked a field goal, and one of the trainers had gotten a sack.

One of my lasting memories of Super Bowl XIX at Stanford came prior to the game. Bill was lying in the middle of the locker room, on the floor, with his head resting on an equipment bag. He was talking to everyone, but no one in particular. He was saying things like, "Yeah, they say Miami has the best quarterback. And the best offense. They even have the best punter. We don't have a chance. We may as well go home now. What do you guys think?"

Said to be a very nice guy off the field, Tom Rathman (wearing a wrist band labeled "Bruise Crew") turned nasty when he put on a uniform.

I can't tell you how much things like that helped relieve tension. The Super Bowl locker room is wild. Guys are kicking things and punching things and hitting each other. There's just a lot more energy in the room as guys put on their Super Bowl "game faces." Some people would actually change personalities right before your eyes. Michael Carter and Tom Rathman immediately come to mind—two of the nicest people in the world, off the field. Strap on the gear and they were the meanest guys on the field.

Bill Parcells talks about players who'll play on concrete in the parking lot if that's where the game will be. Rathman and Carter were like that. Hacksaw Reynolds, too. He wanted to

HOT OFF THE BENCH

Rookie quarterback Clint Longley didn't expect to see much action in 1974, with Roger Staubach in the starter's role coming off a season in which he was the 2nd-ranked quarterback in the NFC. On Thanksgiving Day, though, the Redskins took a 16-3 lead and knocked Staubach out of the game. Longley led the Cowboys back to a 24-23 victory, culminating in a 50-yard touchdown pass to Drew Pearson with 28 seconds left in the game. He would only throw 68 passes in his career, but because he was ready to answer that call, he remains a legend in Dallas to this day.

Despite losing his starting job to NFL star quarterbacks, Joe Montana, John Elway, Steve Young, and Dan Marino, Steve DeBerg threw for 33,872 yards in his career. At the time of his retirement in 1994, DeBerg ranked ninth all-time in passing yards, ahead of names like Simms, Staubach, Jurgensen, Griese, and Blanda.

play and he hated to meet. So when game-morning meetings were established, Hacksaw had his own way of protesting. When I was in a hotel lobby, I saw him coming down the escalator on his way to the meeting—in uniform, already taped up, his helmet snapped.

You do whatever gets you in the right frame of mind, I suppose. I would get to games, as early as I could—I was usually one of the first five guys there. I hated sitting around the hotel waiting. I was at Super Bowl XXIV *six hours* before the game. I wanted to have fun and stay loose, not sit around and let my mind wander. I liked to *prepare*—it helped me be more relaxed on the field.

You can't approach a game any differently whether you're first-string quarterback or third-string clipboard. I had a lot of experience with that early in my career, first with Notre Dame and then with Steve DeBerg in San Francisco. Steve was doing quite well in San Francisco—as he would later do in Denver before John Elway took over, and in Tampa Bay before Steve Young took over. He threw a tighter spiral than I did, but Bill Walsh liked how I threw on the run. So I watched Steve for a year-and-a-half, though I never made any "play me or trade me" demands. All I wanted was a chance, and I eventually got it.

You can't really try to move up if you're the backup. All you can do is be prepared. Eventually you're going to get a chance, but you have to be prepared, or you may never get another one. You need to prepare for each game as if you're the starter. It's going to be that way for awhile. If you're ready, the coaches will see it. Don't complain about not getting a chance and then be unprepared when you finally do. Coaches hate that more than anything.

HEROES IN RESERVE

Don Strock got the call in a January 1982 playoff game in Miami after the San Diego Chargers rolled out to a 24-0 lead in the first quarter. He would throw for nearly 400 yards as he brought the Dolphins back to tie the game. It eventually went to overtime tied at 38-38. The Chargers won the game, but Strock's reputation as a capable "relief pitcher" was reinforced.

In 1990, the Giants were 11-2 and on their way to a playoff showdown with the San Francisco 49ers. Then their starting quarterback, Phil Simms, top-ranked in the NFC, went down with a sprained foot. Backup Jeff Hostetler was in his 7th year in the NFL, but had thrown less than 100 passes. Still he was able to lead the Giants to five straight victories, four by 3 points or less, including a 20-19 victory over the Buffalo Bills in Super Bowl XXV.

THE FINAL GUN

Want to sleep after playing a pro football game? Forget about it. You're sore, you're exhausted, but the excitement is still there. The adrenaline is still running. There's really no easy way to get the adrenaline out of your body, or even to slow it down. Especially if you have a later game. Then sleep will be out of the question. I would lie awake and go through the bad things that happened, thinking about what I would get yelled at for the next day. I'd run the problem through in my mind, process it, and then get ready to hear about it. As I've said before, this is where it really helps to be your own worst critic.

"When you win, you get a feeling of exhilaration. When you lose, you get a feeling of resolution. You resolve never to lose again."

—*Vince Lombardi*

WINNING AND LOSING

You'll win some bad games and you'll lose some good games. You have to find a way to put it all—good or bad—behind you. It's part of the past. There's nothing you can do about it. Everyone makes mistakes. Learn what you can from them and move on. Quarterbacks' mistakes are out there waiting to be seen. They don't stay hidden until they're pointed out by coaches on Monday morning, so you better get used to being visible.

Being able to look ahead and not behind helped me. So did this simple fact: I hate to lose. No, let me rephrase that: **I hate to lose**. Golf, ping pong, tennis, trivia games . . . it doesn't matter.

We all have a competitive side. Using it to your advantage is the first step to succeeding in athletics, but it's a tricky one. You want to win, but you have to realize that a team can't win every game. Just about the worst I've ever felt after a game was at Notre Dame when we lost 27-25 to USC in 1978. We came back from a huge deficit to fall short at the end. Over and over after the game, I kept thinking about how I played in the first half. Around and around in my head: "If I had just played better in the first half. Why didn't I play better in the

"Today and the future are all that count. You spend too much time lingering on what you've done and you get nothing done. There's only one way to coast and that's downhill."

—*Chuck Noll*

REDEMPTION

Quarterback Jim Hardy certainly learned something from a wretched outing in 1950. He was 12 out of 39 passing with eight interceptions and three fumbles in a 45-7 loss. The following week, he threw for six touchdowns in a 55-13 victory.

"Not everyone can be a winner, and if you lose, then you must learn what caused you to lose and how to overcome it. . . . There is nothing wrong with losing, unless you learn to like it."

—*Paul Brown*

Montana walks off the field after watching a 30-20 loss to the Dallas Cowboys in the 1993 NFC Championship game. The 49ers came up short in this contest—it was Montana's last in a 49er uniform—but he left Candlestick Park on the winning end much more often than not.

first half?" You have to accept the losses and learn from the mistakes—although food doesn't taste nearly as good during the days following a loss.

For me, no matter how big or small the game was, winning was good. As long as you won, it kind of evened everything else out. If you lost, it didn't matter how well you played yourself. If you don't care about winning, you don't really care about how you play. You might think you do, but you don't.

HOW YOU PLAY THE GAME

What I'm about to say will sound old-fashioned, but it's what I believe: whether you're winning or losing by a lot or a little, there's no excuse for poor sportsmanship.

I don't like the way it is right now. In the NFL, and in college, it seems as if there is no real respect for anyone or anything. It's "I'm here" and it's "Me." Guys dancing in the end zone—that's fun stuff, I guess, although we didn't do much of it in San Francisco.

I don't know who said it first, but, "when you get to the end zone, act like you've been there before . . . and you'll be back." That's Jerry Rice in a nutshell. Check out Dwight Clark's reaction after he made The Catch against Dallas in the championship game in 1981. Considering the circumstances, it may be the greatest catch anyone has ever made—but he didn't have to strut about it. We knew we had more work to do—namely winning a Super Bowl. Besides, Dwight was too wiped out by the flu to do much dancing anyway.

Now guys make one play, and they take their helmets off and run to the nearest camera. I just don't understand how that is part of the game. A sack, a great catch, a knockdown—these are plays that happen all the time, and there should be some excitement about it, but not to the depths to which it has sunk today. It's gotten out of hand. You even see it in pre-season games. Just do what you have to do, have fun with it, high-five, and get back to business. Keep doing that and you won't have to find the camera. It'll find you.

Remember when Nebraska won their first national title for Tom Osborne against Miami in the Orange Bowl a few

> On running back Marion Motley: "The only statistic he ever knew was whether we won or lost. The man was completely unselfish."
>
> —*Paul Brown*

Despite just throwing a scoring strike in the first half of Super Bowl XIX, Montana remains under control, knowing his business is yet unfinished.

years ago? Miami's defense was exhausted in the 4th quarter, and they sure could have used a lot of the energy they spent in the 1st quarter yanking off their helmets and screaming after every tackle. Fortunately, the NCAA passed a rule the following season to make players keep their helmets on. Seems to me that a coach shouldn't need a rule like that to keep his players from acting like clowns. Interestingly, the NFL passed the same rule before the 1997 season.

Sometimes it spills over from college to the pros. We've had rookies come to camp and show absolutely no respect for ten-year veterans. Many think everything should be given to them, as opposed to having to earn respect on the field. I was taught that the only way to earn anything is on the field.

OFF THE FIELD

As tough as I was on myself after a game, I was always very easy on my opposition. You don't want anything you say to end up on someone else's bulletin board. Win or lose, you should show respect for the opposition—and be upbeat about your own team, because your teammates may be reading what you have to say. Athletes are getting criticized these days for speaking in clichés and measuring everything they say, but you have to do that to some extent. The press want you to say something to stir things up, while you're doing everything you can to stay out of trouble. Some players have actually been accused of being intentionally dull in the hope that the media will give up and leave them alone.

Bill Walsh had explicit instructions for his players in terms of dealing with the media. He had already learned his lessons by the time we arrived. He taught us that we didn't always have to be Mr. Quotable to get along with the media, but you can still get burned. There are just enough bad guys who want to say something critical about you, or who have another agenda than actually telling the story properly. We learned to always be on guard for this.

Unfortunately, the media and the public may only see one side of a player. It was a long time before they clued in to the fact that the 49ers were a bunch of pranksters, because the players tended to be so guarded around the press. Growing up in public is not easy. The worst thing that ever happened to me was when a columnist attacked my wife and me for having a baby during the season. This when five other 49ers' babies were born during that season—and mine was the only one born on a day off! Still, I get ripped for having "bad timing." That's about the time I stopped reading newspapers.

Joe learned to cope with media attention during his amateur playing days at Notre Dame.

"The exposure here is tremendous, but so is the pressure to perform. There are probably many more people watching what I do each week, and what the team does, than with most other schools."

—*Joe Montana at Notre Dame*

The press is just one of the off-field obstacles that a quarterback has to deal with. Playing at Notre Dame was a good preparation for the fishbowl life of a professional athlete. It was a tough school academically, but there was also a lot of pressure to win. The alumni demanded it, and the young players knew the tradition and wanted to uphold it: Daryle Lamonica, John Huarte, Terry Hanratty, Joe Theismann. And those were just the quarterbacks from the 15 years before I got there.

Quarterbacks must get accustomed to living under the proverbial microscope, whether it's on the field during a Super Bowl, walking to class on a college campus, or even leaving a high school stadium. Make no mistake, this is not an easy thing to deal with. There are some ways, however, to cope with it. You have to establish a separation between your public and private lives. Nobody else will do it for you. If you don't set the ground rules early, the situation will just get worse, and your public life will just keep invading your private life. You have to find a way to not let the well-wishers interfere with other things you want to do while you're out in public.

Getting a lot of attention from the public starts in high school. Everyone watches the quarterback, whether it's in class or in the hallway. This simply expands at the collegiate and then professional level. The real fishbowl effect starts in college, though, especially at the football powers. Even at a small college, there's going to be a lot of attention. You have to learn how to handle the pressure.

There will be all kinds of pressure. Do you get stage fright because the game is on television? Why? How do you know you're on television, anyway? You can't see the cameras while you're on the field. If you're looking at the camera, you're in the wrong business. Are you annoyed because the media are always there? Well, there'll be times when you're glad they are. It's all part of the package, so either you find a way to deal with it or you don't survive. Are you tired of all the attention you're getting from fans? Get used to that, too. Unless you want that attention to get awfully negative, remember the Golden Rule: do unto others as you would have them do unto you. The best thing to do in this situation is to be yourself. The same, all the time.

Joe Montana speaks at his farewell rally in downtown San Francisco in April 1995. More than 25,000 49ers fans attended to bid their farewell.

FINAL SECONDS

If you've gotten this far, I must not have scared you off completely. I hope that this book will help you be a better quarterback. For the coaches and parents, I hope this will help you encourage your children to be the best they can be at whatever they choose to do. For the football fans, I hope this will help you gain a greater appreciation for what the quarterback—and really the entire offensive unit—has to contend with every weekend. And for anyone else who's listened in, I hope you can find something in how people approach this game that will inspire you in your own endeavors.

To paraphrase Paul Brown, *that* will be the test of where we've finished.

"The test of a quarterback is where his team finishes."

—*Paul Brown*

120 Years of Football in 10 Minutes

Watch an NFL game today and you might see teams using the pass to set up the run . . . lining up with one running back . . . two tight ends or none at all . . . three, four, or sometimes five wide receivers. How did we get here?

Football has been an ongoing struggle between offense and defense, not just on the field but on the blackboard. Coaches have been devising strategies—and counter-tactics—for 120 years. Knowing how the offense evolved to its present state can help you better understand *why* things are done a certain way today.

Walter Camp is credited with inventing American football in 1876 at Yale. But it took awhile for this game to even begin to resemble what we call football today. For example, it wasn't until 1880 that the line of scrimmage was established, until 1881 that downs were used, and until 1887 that it was legal to tackle someone below the knees. In fact, it wasn't even until 1912 that a touch-down was six points and a field goal three points—or that four downs and ten yards to go, a 100-yard field, and a legal forward pass were part of the game.

A famous day in football history is November 1, 1913, when Notre Dame's Gus Dorais threw 17 passes, completing 13—most to a guy named Knute Rockne—for 243 yards passing to beat Army 35-13. It would be several more years before passes were viewed as anything more than trick plays, but Notre Dame showed what could be done by putting the ball in the air.

Professional football began to get organized in the 1920s, although 49 different teams came and went during the decade. Familiar names such as the Green Bay Packers, Chicago Bears, and New York Giants were taking the field. So too were the Muncie Flyers, Tonawanda Kardex, Providence Steam Roller, and New York Yankees. So if you think today's franchise movements are confusing, they've got nothing on the '20s.

Back then, Packers' coach Curly Lambeau actually threw the ball some—but mostly it was single-wing football in the '20s. In this two-tight-end-formation, the quarterback was actually lined up behind a tackle, his primary responsibility was blocking, and the snap went directly to the fullback. Imagine a fake punt where the ball is snapped to the upback, or a shotgun formation with the ball going directly to Daryl Johnston—that's pretty much what it was. The single wing had four men in the backfield, stacked to one side, and those teams that ran it relied on power and blocking to be effective—outnumbering the defense at the point of attack, with the runner heading to a spot called in the huddle (by those teams that used a huddle!) But plays were slow to develop, long runs were rarely broken, and the defense had little to fear from the possibility of a pass. This was the original three-yards-and-a-cloud-of-dust offense.

A series of rules changes made passing a more viable option in the '30s. Hashmarks were established in 1932, and it took a winter blizzard to do it. The league's inaugural championship game was to be played in Wrigley Field, but extreme weather forced it inside. It was played in Chicago Stadium, home of hockey's Black Hawks and later Michael Jordan's Chicago Bulls. Because of the tight quarters, some changes had to be made. For example, back then the ball was snapped from where the previous play ended. Because the sidelines were right up against the hockey boards, hashmarks were placed ten yards from each sideline. When plays went out-of-bounds, the next snap was taken on the nearest hashmark—an idea that stuck, with necessity yet again the mother of invention.

> "Will it work in the NFL? Sure it might. For a weekend."
>
> —Buddy Ryan, Chicago Bears defensive coordinator, on the run-and-shoot in 1985

Rules that punished incompletions—an incompletion into the end zone was essentially the same as a punt, and it was a five-yard penalty to throw two incompletions in the same series of downs—were loosened. Most importantly, the roundish ball was tapered to make it easier to grip and throw. In this new environment, Curly Lambeau's Packers thrived. They lined up in formations that closely resemble today's pro set, with ends split wide. Pass patterns were reinvented, now that they had a fast rookie end named Don Hutson running them. He would go on to catch a pass in 95 consecutive games, a record that would stand for 24 years.

The next major innovation was the T-formation of the Bears, where the quarterback lined up directly behind the center. Legend has it, this formation was unveiled against the Redskins in the 1940 championship game—and that Bears quarterback, Sid Luckman, would actually weep when it was drawn up and showed to him. It was a game that Chicago would go on to win 73-0. Actually, the Redskins had beaten the Bears and their T earlier in the season. But success is imitated in sport, and during the '40s nearly every NFL team would abandon the predictable single-wing for the deception of the T-formation.

Running backs were now coached to find a hole, rather than run to the preordained spot where the blocking advantage would be. The quarterback was no longer a blocker—he did his part for the running game not by blocking but by passing effectively, the threat of the pass keeping some defenders further from the point of attack. Successful running would invariably cause the defense to overplay it, opening up the opportunity for

a big pass play—the birth of using-the-run-to-establish-the-pass. Quickness was suddenly catching up to power as an offensive weapon.

In 1949, the first pro set was run—one tight end, a split end, two running backs, and the third running back up close to the line of scrimmage as a second wide receiver. Meanwhile in a rival league called the All-America Football Conference, a coach named Paul Brown (whose disciples would include Bill Walsh) was introducing the concept of the pocket to his offensive line and blocking backs. And in the much more complicated offense that the T-formation allowed, he wanted more control. He called all the plays, not the quarterback, relaying them to the huddle via messenger.

Now it was time for the defense to adapt and adjust. Before the T, most teams played a 7-1-3 defense designed to stack men on the line of scrimmage and stop the run. With the threat of the pass, defenders had to play further back from the line. That led to the 5-2-4 of the Eagles, which would return about twenty years later as the 3-4. The Giants developed what was then called the 6-1-4, which met the deception of the T-formation with deception of its own. The ends might play the run or drop into coverage, a formation that would evolve into today's 4-3 defense with these ends now called outside linebackers.

With the 4-3 came the middle linebacker, a position that demanded both power and speed—and with it also came the blitz, with linebackers, often unblocked, going all out for the quarterback on passing plays. So when offenses would later be victimized by the power, speed, and bad attitudes of Sam Huff,

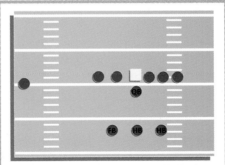

The original T-formation actually had three offensive players in the backfield. This formation baffled defenses for a while, until they countered with the 5-2-4, which later evolved into the 3-4 defense.

Dick Butkus, or Ray Nitschke, they would have to remember that these were monsters of their own creation.

In the 1960s, Green Bay's Vince Lombardi resurrected the single-wing—only this time it was called the power sweep, the blocking led not by the quarterback and halfback but by pulling guards. Packer linemen "option blocked," going with the defender rather than trying to redirect him, and leaving it up to the ball-carrier to "run to daylight." No deception here; the defense knew what was coming, but few could stop it. Tom Landry's Cowboys came closest to containing the Packers sweeps and misdirection plays, relying on a "flex" defense where a defensive tackle and defensive end played off the line and moved laterally, rather than taking the blockers head on.

Lombardi's system won, so that was what the other NFL teams imitated. But things couldn't have been more different in a rival league called the American Football League. The coach of the San Diego Chargers, Sid Gillman, came up with a high-powered offense built on speedy receivers who could go deep and run precise routes, and quarterbacks who could throw deep and hit receivers on the break. This was called "stretching the defense," a concept later embraced by Al Davis's Raiders, Chuck Noll's Steelers, and Don Coryell's Chargers. Gillman wasn't the only innovator in the AFL; Kansas City coach Hank Stram introduced a moving pocket to his offensive scheme, with quarterback Len Dawson able to roll out and throw without abandoning his protection. He also had some success with the I-formation, where the halfback and fullback lined up directly behind the quarterback. Because of the alignment of the blocking back, this formation made it harder for the defense to tell which way a running play was designed to go. Since the halfback was lined up so much deeper, it gave him more time to read the defense and set up his blocks.

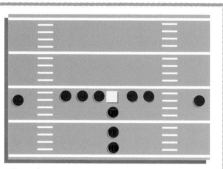

The I-formation helped veil the ground attack. With two backs, it was harder for the defense to tell who would be running the football and which direction the play was going.

The NFL and AFL merged in 1970, but the high-powered AFL offenses did not come along. In fact, if you look at a top ten list of the highest scoring pro teams, none played during the '70s. Most teams were playing it conservative on defense, relying more and more on the zone defense—where defensive backs and linebackers were responsible for regions of the field rather than a specific receiver. Teams like the Dolphins and Steelers won with defense and rushing, and the occasional bomb to Paul Warfield or Lynn Swann to keep the defenses honest. With stopping the run of paramount importance, the 3-4 returned.

But, like the '30s, rules changes were the passing game's best friend. The penalty for holding was reduced from 15 yards to 10. To reduce the number of field goals, the goal posts were moved to the back of the end zone. The hashmarks were moved in for the fourth time, to give more room for ends to run routes. Defensive backs were no longer allowed to play bump-and-run coverage, now allowed only one con-tact with the receiver within five yards of the line of scrimmage. The head slap was banished from the defensive linemen's repertoire, while offensive linemen were now allowed to pass-block with open hands.

The effect of these rules changes wasn't felt until the early '80s, but when they did finally take hold they ushered in an era of unprecedented passing success. The Chargers and Redskins went to one-back formations with two tight ends—one a blocker, the other a pass catcher. The vertical passing game of the Chargers and Raiders of the '60s gave way to the more horizontal, possession passing game—the "West Coast offense"—introduced by the 49ers. Some called these short passes basically "long handoffs," with rhythm and timing essential to making it work. In the history of the NFL, only Steve Young and Joe Montana have completed more than 60% of their passes and had fewer than 3% of their passes picked off—a tribute to this system.

The defense responded to the offensive surge in two ways. Lawrence Taylor reinvented the outside linebacker position, lining up wide, primarily as a pass rusher. Soon nearly every team had a speed-rushing outside linebacker coming from the quarterback's blindside. (Since most quarterbacks are righthanded, the left tackle is responsible for protecting the blindside—which is why you're starting to see the best ones getting paid what they deserve.) Chicago Bears defensive coordinator, Buddy Ryan, created the 46 Defense—a defense that was designed to put maximum pressure on the quarterback, rather than let him sit back in the pocket and pick the secondary apart. Sometimes seven men rushed the quarterback, while eight men were often at the line of scrimmage to stuff the run. Defensive players were now good enough athletes that they could rush the passer hard and still be able to stop the run if that's what came their way. It was a high-risk approach, but when it worked, the offense was completely overwhelmed.

Some teams fought pressure with pressure, responding to the fierce pass rushing with quick-hitting plays and more speed on the offensive side of the ball. Ironically perhaps, the best way to beat a heavy pass rush was to throw more. The Bills went to four consecutive Super Bowls by frequently using one back, one tight end, and three wide receivers—and combatting the defense's situational substitutions by going without a huddle. The Houston Oilers, Detroit Lions, and later the Atlanta Falcons took this approach to the extreme, abandoning the tight end completely to go with four wide receivers. It was called the run-and-shoot, a product of the rival United States Football League, and it required the receivers to run quick routes, reading the defense along with the quarterback and reacting accordingly. Completion percentages went up, though yards per completion did not.

Defenses struggled at first to figure out how to play against three wide receiver sets and the run-and-shoot. Some tried five and six defensive backs. Those that were most successful simply applied pressure—pounding the smaller receivers when they came over the middle, rushing the quarterback relentlessly to force him into making a mistake or knock him out of the game.

Now, in the late '90s, there is the zone blitz. It used to be that when a quarterback read zone coverage at the line, he at least knew he'd probably have some time to throw. And that when he read blitz, he'd at least have man-to-man coverage he could try to beat. Not anymore. Defenses are focusing on confusing a quarterback's reads, even if it means dropping defensive linemen into pass coverage or bringing blitzes that leave large holes in zone coverage. Like everything else, most offenses will figure out how to beat the zone blitz eventually.

In fact, these offenses will probably figure out several ways to do it, because there is more than one way to move the ball. A quick look at the recent Super Bowl winners reveals many different offensive approaches. The West Coast Offense of the 49ers and the Packers (coached by Walsh disciples, George Seifert and Mike Holmgren) using the pass to establish the run. The Cowboys using the run to establish the pass. The Giants' low-risk approach of using the run to establish the run—eating the clock, holding onto the ball, and wearing out the defense. The only constant was execution.

There's no defense against that.

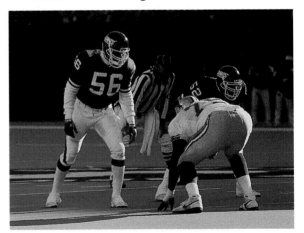

Lawrence Taylor changed the game of football with his sheer power and blazing speed coming off the line. LT lined up wide and on the line of scrimmage, striking fear in the hearts of opposing quarterbacks.

Recommended Reading

The Gamemakers by Jack Clary
No Medal for Trying by Jerry Izenberg
Inside the Helmet by Peter King
The Thinking Man's Guide to Pro Football by Paul Zimmerman

Special Acknowledgments

The authors would like to acknowledge the special editorial and design/production contributions of Mountain Lion, Inc., a book developer/producer that specializes in bringing sports books to market. The following individuals helped to bring about the creation of *Joe Montana's Art and Magic of Quarterbacking.* To all of them we say, "Thanks."

- Doug Myers, editor, who conducted supplementary interviews and research, wrote the sidebar and "120 Years of Football in 10 Minutes," and worked with the authors to produce the final text.
- Kim Habel, illustrator; Margaret Trejo of Trejo Production, typesetting and design.
- Mark Gola, managing editor, who shepherded the project and wrote the captions for the photographs; Melissa Martin, copyeditor.
- Matthew J. Lee, Larry French, and Jon Naso photographers; Joanna Bruno, sales representative, AP Wide World Photos; John Heisler, Sports Information Director, Notre Dame University.

INDEX